T0146625

DOLLAR IMPLOSION!

RETURN OF THE GOLD STANDARD

KAYA COLAK

 iUniverse®

DOLLAR IMPLOSION!
RETURN OF THE GOLD STANDARD

iUniverse books may be ordered through booksellers or by contacting:

*iUniverse
1663 Liberty Drive
Bloomington, IN 47403
www.iuniverse.com
1-800-Authors (1-800-288-4677)*

*Because of the dynamic nature of the Internet, any web addresses or links contained in
this book may have changed since publication and may no longer be valid. The views
expressed in this work are solely those of the author and do not necessarily reflect the
views of the publisher, and the publisher hereby disclaims any responsibility for them.*

*Any people depicted in stock imagery provided by Getty Images are models,
and such images are being used for illustrative purposes only.
Certain stock imagery © Getty Images.*

*ISBN: 978-1-5320-6541-5 (sc)
ISBN: 978-1-5320-6542-2 (e)*

Print information available on the last page.

iUniverse rev. date: 02/04/2019

DEDICATION

I dedicate this book to my wife, Elenis, and to my five children, Sema, Ozan, Nilay, Nerya, and Nayla. You are and will always be the true source of inspiration in my life. Thank you for your love and support always.

PREFACE

This book is a work of fiction. However, it is also an historic analysis and a completely plausible scenario of the future based on current trends...

At various times in my life, I have wanted to write a book about one topic or another. Now, as a "middle-aged" man, I have finally decided that I have an important gift to give to the world. I hope that readers of this book will take heed and prepare for the massive economic and political changes I foresee in this decade and the next.

I have been extremely fortunate in my life. Not only was I born and raised in the wealthiest nation on earth, but I also had the good fortune of growing up in a loving family in an affluent suburb of Detroit, Michigan.

On some level, I have always believed that my personal life experience was a microcosm of the United States of America. This is because my parents immigrated to the United States to carve out a better life for themselves and their children—they were living the American Dream! I am their oldest child and much was expected of me. I was an excellent student and was voted "Most Outstanding Boy" of West Hills Junior High School. I was at the top of my class in high school which happened to be one of the best public school systems in the country.

My hard work paid off when I gained acceptance to Stanford University. After graduating from Stanford in only three years, I was accepted to medical school at Wayne State University in Detroit,

Michigan. I successfully completed medical school and then served five years in the Diagnostic Radiology Residency Training Program at the Wayne State University/Detroit Medical Center. I even found time to get married during the last month of my residency. I went on to complete subspecialty training in Vascular and Interventional Radiology at the University of Tennessee—Memphis and MRI Fellowship at Michigan State University. My life was literally a fairy tale out of a storybook.

However, just as there are villains and mishaps in a fairy tale, I endured several unexpected mishaps of my own. Divorce and treachery in the workplace are two of those bumps that I have encountered along the road of life.

In this book, Johnny is the allegorical character representing the United States of America. But in a very real sense, *I am Johnny* because I believe my life epitomizes the American Dream. Please do not begrudge my use of poetic license with respect to Johnny. My intention is not to deceive the reader, but merely to paint as vivid a picture as possible.

My personal financial Armageddon occurred in late 2007 when I went through a painful divorce that ultimately led to the foreclosure on my home, the loss of rental properties, and the loss of my retirement account and entire life savings--resulting in tens of thousands of dollars in legal bills.

Unfortunately, the real estate bubble burst right around the time of the divorce proceedings. The marital home was on the market for over eighteen months, but did not get a single offer. I had no choice but to let the home go into foreclosure. We lost all of our equity in the home in the process. I was going bankrupt and nobody was there to bail me out!

Needless to say, I learned volumes about legal and financial matters during this process. I learned that all of the real estate investments I had made were bad ones. More accurately, I had bought the home and two rental properties by making a down payment of roughly 20 percent. The problem was that the bank owned 80 percent of the properties. So I was working almost solely for the bank and didn't realize it.

This was a formula for disaster because any major setback such as divorce, accident, or illness could lead to losing everything. Shockingly, when I fell behind on my mortgage payments, the bank demanded payment in full for *all* of my outstanding loans. I swore never to buy any real estate again with less than a 50 percent down payment.

I then moved to Florida to start my life anew. Three years after the divorce was final, I received a letter in the mail from a law firm claiming they had a judgment in their possession for $65,000! I could not believe my eyes.

I read the letter carefully. I then remembered that the bank had won a judgment against me for $50,000 and then sold the judgment to a collection agency. The collection agency had apparently piled on interest and attorney fees, reaching a grand total of over $65,000. The collection agency then hired a legal firm to garnish my wages which was finally completed in 2011. The bank was ruthless and I was powerless against the vastly more powerful bank and its surrogates.

Out of this experience and an emotionally painful episode of treachery in the workplace sprang the creation of my first website, wikiadvocate.com, which was originally conceived as a social support network for those in personal crisis. The original goal of the website was sharing life's difficulties and supporting others with sound advice. It has since morphed into a site advocating the interests of the "little guy" vis-à-vis large organizations and institutions.

We are witnessing the integration of social networks like Facebook and LinkedIn into the fabric of our lives. I now see the creation of an individual empowerment society right before my eyes. However, this trend is part of a much larger transformation in human history—a paradigm shift from the Industrial Age to the **"Age of the Individual**," a term I have coined. American physicist, David Bohm, has brilliantly and elegantly proposed the "holographic paradigm" to describe the philosophical underpinnings of the new paradigm, the **Age of the Individual**.

We have also seen the power of the Internet to drive influential movements in society, including the brilliantly orchestrated election of Barack Obama as President of the United States, the Occupy movement and President Donald Trump's incessant utilization of Twitter. From 2011 onward, we witnessed the "Arab Awakening," in which the people revolted against their dictators in Tunisia, Egypt, Libya, Yemen, Bahrain, and Syria.

Here in the United States, I believe our political system needs a third party that is "socially liberal and fiscally conservative." Jesse "the Body" Ventura, the former pro wrestler and governor of the state of Minnesota, came close in his views and policies, but the movement seemed to fizzle out. The rise of the Tea Party and the Occupy movement come close, but neither has yet risen to the status of a viable third party force in American politics.

Interestingly, retired Congressman Ron Paul of Texas, a Libertarian, seems to represent the views of radical change so desperately needed today. His son, Senator Rand Paul of Kentucky, could be the voice of a new ideology in American politics. I am not advocating classical libertarianism, which will ultimately lead to chaos and an unworkable society. Rather, I am simply espousing a "socially liberal, fiscally conservative" political movement that will propel society forward. I believe that this political perspective will gain strength in the coming years, far beyond anyone's expectations.

I was inspired by the books *Aftershock*, by Wiedemer, Wiedemer, and Spitzer, which showed me that our dollar-based economy is being transformed into a more equitable economic system based on gold, and *Wikinomics*, by Tapscott and Williams, demonstrating that our collective future is collaborative and that everybody contributes to it.

I strongly believe in the viewpoint espoused by Dr. Wiedemer, that ours is a "Bubble Economy," and that we have witnessed the bursting of the real estate, stock market, private equity, and discretionary spending bubbles beginning in late 2008 and continuing into the present. The final bubbles to burst are the intertwined ideas of the dollar bubble and the government debt bubble.

I have been influenced by the growing "gold and silver stacker" or "prepper" movement on the Internet. This movement or school of thought believes that the United States is headed toward some type of economic catastrophe due to unsustainable debt and corruption of the federal government led by the banker cabal and that one of the main ways to prepare for this event is to buy gold and silver bars and coins.

Jim Willie, Ph.D. who writes a newsletter called The Hat Trick Letter on his website, www.goldenjackass.com, seems to be one of the most insightful of these bloggers. He boldly claims that the US dollar in its current form, the Federal Reserve Note, will no longer be accepted by the rest of the world forcing the US government to create a new US Treasury dollar which will ultimately be devalued by 70%! His work centers on how this transition from the US dollar to Gold as the world's reserve currency will take place.

Finally, my initial foray into the concept of individual empowerment began back in the 1980's when my fraternity brother and I created and produced a 6-hour audiocassette program entitled *Insight into the New Age*, by Willis Harman, Ph.D. We truly believed that we were helping to usher in the "New Age" of enlightenment. The entire crux of the audio program was a simple, yet profound shift in paradigm or worldview: "**the primacy of inner conscious awareness as a causal reality.**" This means that each and every one of us creates our own reality with our thoughts!

The most recent influence on my thinking is from a book entitled, *The Law of Attraction* by Esther and Jerry Hicks. In this book, Esther Hicks channels a group of Non-physical beings named Abraham. Abraham describes the "rules of the game of life" to the reader as follows: "The most powerful Law in the Universe, the Law of Attraction, simply states: that which is like unto itself is drawn." If you believe and understand this Law, you can focus your thoughts on what you would like to attract into your experience and take your attention away from those things that you do not desire.

Once you internalize the Law of Attraction, you can then go on to utilize the second and third Laws of the Universe, the Science of Deliberate Creation and the Art of Allowing. The Science of Deliberate Creation states, "That which I give thought to and that which I believe or expect—is." The Art of Allowing simply states, "I am that which I am and I am allowing all others to be that which they are."

The concepts in this book are very powerful and can be life-changing. However, you do not have to rely on the words or thoughts in this book. By simply observing the current "Dollar Implosion" and collapse of the current monetary system with the dollar as the world's reserve currency giving way to the "Return of the Gold Standard," you are witnessing an historic event of biblical proportions.

This paradigm shift in the world of economics is a metaphor for the larger paradigm shift in our collective worldview—the **Age of the Individual**. This new worldview emphatically states that you can begin to create the future that you desire by directing your thoughts first and foremost to what you desire and what feels good—then aligning with those thoughts and desires.

The empowerment of the individual is driving the change to a more fair and equitable economic system for humanity. From the ashes of the old deterministic system will emerge a new society based on the empowerment of the individual with respect for the rights and welfare of all living beings.

Kaya Colak
November 2018

TABLE OF CONTENTS

ACT I

THE RISE AND FALL OF
THE AMERICAN EMPIRE

CHAPTER 1

ALL EMPIRES RISE AND FALL. . .
OURS IS NO EXCEPTION

I am going to use a simple analogy throughout this book to tell the story of global economic development. Imagine each of the world's nations to be a single individual at the stage of life corresponding to their phase of economic development. We, the United States of America, would be a strong man about forty-five years of age, named Johnny. . .

Cast of Characters:

Johnny	United States of America
Karl	Germany
Nicholas	France
Oliver	England
Alexander	Russia
Wojciech	Poland
Minjoon	South Korea
Nguyen	Vietnam
Hiroto	Japan
Chen	China
Frank	Confederate South (prior to the United States Civil War)
David	Israel
Johnny's wife	Saudi Arabia
"The Bank"	International Banking Cartel
Ashish	India
Carlos	Brazil
Mehmet	Turkey
Laszlo	Hungary
Czech	Czechoslovakia
Mohammed	Tunisia
Hassan	Egypt
Ali	Libya
Malik	Pakistan

Johnny's mother and father had immigrated to Canada from the Old World, to seek a better life for themselves. Johnny's father always had his eye on the United States. He was a physician and had spent five years of his life serving internship and residency in the field of internal medicine in five different locations in the United States.

Johnny's father grew up during the war and lived at a subsistence level during those years, as did much of the developing world. So Johnny's father jumped from one residency training program to another, five times in five years, because the next program offered a few dollars more pay per year.

Then Johnny's mother became pregnant with him. With Johnny's mother nine months pregnant, his mother and father legally crossed the border from Windsor, Ontario in Canada, to Detroit, Michigan. They stayed at the cheapest motel they could find on Woodward Avenue, the Oak Motel, for six dollars per night. Three days later, on August 7, 1966, Johnny was born (**Birth of the United States of America on July 4, 1776**).

Johnny had an idyllic childhood. When he was just three years old, his mother took him to the park one hot summer day. Johnny saw some kids who were older than him playing with a ball. He couldn't speak yet, but he knew he wanted that ball. So he simply walked up to one of the boys who had the ball, pushed him down, and took it. From that day on, Johnny knew he was special, and he learned that brute force wins the day.

Johnny grew to be big and strong. He was the tallest boy in his class throughout elementary school. He was also one of the brightest. But Johnny also had more than his share of fights with other children. The other children teased him because of his immigrant heritage and he kept trying to prove himself to them. But deep down inside,

Johnny knew he was gifted and had a special role to play on the stage of life (**Manifest Destiny—the 19th century American belief that the United States was destined to expand across the continent and spread Western civilization throughout the New World**).

When Johnny was in third grade, he got into a big fight during *recess with another boy, Frank, who was in the fifth grade (**American Civil War**). All the kids circled around Johnny and Frank and began shouting, "Fight! Fight! Fight!"*

The two boys took a few swings at each other, then grabbed each other and fell to the ground. Johnny had been taking wrestling lessons and was able to pin Frank down to the ground. Johnny sat on top of Frank and could have hurt him badly, but then decided to let Frank go.

By that time, the teacher on recess duty had arrived to see what was happening, and she was shocked. She promptly took both boys by the wrist and marched them down to the principal's office. From that day on, Johnny became the hero of his school.

Johnny was blessed with loving parents, siblings, and relatives, and he had the good fortune to go to the best schools in town. He was an excellent student, a gifted athlete, and a talented trumpet player in the school band and orchestra. He was voted Most Outstanding Boy of the ninth grade at his school.

*In his junior year of high school, Johnny won First Prize in the annual science competition with his original research on atomic physics (**Atomic Bomb**). By the time he came of age, he was the strongest young man in the neighborhood (**The United States becomes the wealthiest, most powerful nation on earth**). Whenever anybody needed help, Johnny would gladly oblige.*

When Johnny was just twenty-five years old, he learned that his dear friends in the next neighborhood, Karl, Nicholas, Oliver and others in that circle, had a terrible falling out. It seems each one yearned to be the "king of the hill" and could not bear to see another in charge of the neighborhood.

*The whole situation quickly escalated and led to a huge brawl (**World War II**). Karl was the instigator of the brawl and most everybody else was trying to defend himself against the strong and powerful Karl. Some would even say Karl was a megalomaniac (**Nazi Germany**).*

All of the townspeople began to gather around this incredible spectacle. Everybody in town thought that these young men would end up destroying each other. Karl began his reign of terror by first picking on the weakest of the bunch, Wojciech, and giving him a good old-fashioned beating (**German invasion of Poland in 1939**). Everybody knew that Wojciech was simply no match for the stronger, ruthless Karl. Beaten down and bruised, poor Wojciech ran home crying.

Then Karl set his sights on Nicholas and Oliver. He pushed Nicholas to the ground. Nicholas got back on his feet and put up a good fight. But the stronger Karl beat him into submission. Karl and Oliver got into skirmishes, too. But Oliver had special talent in the field of aerial acrobatics, so Oliver managed to escape Karl's powerful knockout punches. Then there was David. Karl was much bigger and stronger than David and he perpetually teased him and beat him up (**Holocaust**).

In the neighboring town, a young man named Alexander was just twenty years old and was also coming of age. He was the leader of his neighborhood gang and heard about horrible Karl. Alexander decided to investigate for himself. Alexander saw Karl in the street one day, and went right up to his face and said, "If you think you're a real man, then try to beat me up!"

Karl became irate and brandished a shiny knife! Alexander was prepared and miraculously produced his own shiny weapon. They circled around each other like two cobras poised to attack each other. Alexander stumbled and nearly fell to the ground. Karl lunged toward Alexander and stabbed him repeatedly. Alexander fell to the ground and bled profusely. He miraculously crawled away to safety, barely managing to escape with his life. But deep down inside, Alexander knew he would make Karl pay for this dastardly deed (**Eastern Front of World War II**).

Alexander and Karl fought repeatedly. How much pain and suffering could either man take? Finally, the townspeople asked the mighty Johnny if he would break up the fight. Johnny reluctantly agreed. Johnny had the strength of an ox and was clever as a fox. He had become a legend in his neighborhood and everybody loved him. Even his foes admired him.

One day when Alexander and Karl were slugging it out, Johnny decided to put an end to this rivalry once and for all. He summoned up his incredible strength and single-handedly knocked Karl out with an awesome blow to the head and body (**D-Day**). *Karl was out cold lying motionless on the ground. When he finally got up, he vowed never to bully anyone as long as he lived. Johnny was the hero of the town!*

But he didn't stop there. Hiroto had launched a surprise attack on Johnny destroying his favorite yacht several months ago (**Attack on Pearl Harbor on December 7, 1941**). *Then Hiroto threatened Johnny and the entire neighborhood and vowed that he would not stop until Johnny was defeated. Johnny had no choice but to unleash his secret weapon on Hiroto* (**Atomic Bombs dropped on Hiroshima and Nagasaki, Japan on August 6th and 9th, 1945**). *Hiroto's entire estate was leveled to the ground. He instantly surrendered and also vowed never to bully again.*

After all this fighting, Karl, Nicholas and Oliver were left weak and debilitated. Johnny decided to help Karl, Nicholas, and Oliver rebuild their strength, and he showed them how to train properly to stay in the best possible shape (**Marshall Plan**). *He now made the rules, and all the other boys in the neighborhood had to follow those rules* (**Bretton Woods Agreement**).

Several months later, the battle-weary bear-like Alexander walked into the neighborhood and challenged Johnny to a fight. They argued and postured for a long time, but then agreed to postpone their fight for another time.

They both went home and began to train for the big battle. They built up their muscles and became amazingly strong. They also enlisted the support of everybody they could find to join the fight on their respective sides (**The Cold War**). *This went on for a long time. All of the townspeople thought that this stalemate would continue forever.*

Johnny and Alexander kept bumping heads. One time they came so close to annihilating each other that everybody in the whole town became terrified (**Cuban Missile Crisis**). *The two strong giants had gotten into a nasty brawl. Alexander pulled out a shiny switchblade. Johnny* *pulled out a machete. They faced each other squarely with weapon in hand waiting for the other to strike first. It seemed as if there was no way out but to attack the other. Each was determined to fight to the death.*

*Then, out of the blue, lightning struck them both and they fell to the ground. They took this as an omen from God and quickly agreed to stop the fight while still managing to save face with their compatriots. This tense relationship continued for several years longer. They constantly threatened to kill each other, but neither one ever did (**"MAD"—the doctrine of Mutually Assured Destruction**).*

*As Johnny got older, he challenged other weaker teenagers and young men to fights. He once fought a young man named Minjoon (**Korean War**). It was a painful fight that didn't go as easily as planned. Johnny emerged victorious, but ended up with a black eye. Then Johnny fought a teenager named Nguyen, who was so unbelievably tough that Johnny almost lost the fight (**Vietnam War**). In fact, Johnny received a few flesh wounds after being stabbed several times. But Johnny eventually won the fight. He even dated a few of Nguyen's sisters along the way.*

*Meanwhile, Alexander was busy making friends with Czech (**Czechoslovakia**), Wojiech (**Poland**), Laszlo (**Hungary**), and others. Alexander was stronger than any of them, so Alexander made the rules, and they obliged (**Iron Curtain of Eastern Europe**). But Alexander had his share of problems too. One day, Czech rose up and challenged Alexander to a fight (**Prague Revolt of 1968**). It was a spectacle! Alexander won the fight, but was badly hurt. He never fully recovered his old strength after that fight.*

Alexander was also living a very lavish life. He was spending all his money on weights, dumbbells, protein supplements, and energy drinks, but he really was not eating too healthy. He also spent money that he didn't have by maxing out his credit cards.

*Eventually, Alexander became so unproductive that he simply could not pay his bills. He just didn't have the same strength that he'd had in his twenties. At the age of forty, Alexander declared bankruptcy and most all of Alexander's closest friends began to desert him one by one (**Collapse of Soviet Union**).*

Now Johnny was the king of the whole neighborhood once again. It seemed that he had unlimited strength. His reputation extended far and wide. Johnny felt invincible and deservedly so.

Johnny was an entrepreneur, too. He single-handedly built the world's largest automobile factory, Universal Motors Corporation. His factory epitomized the age of automation. He worked very hard and became incredibly successful. Johnny was selling his cars and the American way of life to the world.

Soon, the whole world was emulating Johnny's model of success. In fact, Johnny single-handedly helped build the largest middle class the world has ever seen. The working man had triumphed over the aristocracy.

Unfortunately for Johnny, the fairy tale does not end here. Johnny learned that there were adolescents in his neighborhood, Alexander's neighborhood and other neighborhoods, who had also grown big and strong.

*Chen (**China**), Ashish (**India**), Carlos (**Brazil**), Mehmet (**Turkey**), and others now wanted to rule their own neighborhoods. Meanwhile, Hiroto (**Japan**) and Minjoon (**South Korea**) were busy building automobile factories of their own. In fact, their cars rivaled and even surpassed Johnny's in quality and value. This is where Johnny finds himself today…*

THE STORY OF THE AMERICAN EMPIRE

This is the unfolding story of the economic development of the world. Human history is filled with the stories of vast empires that dominated the Earth, including the Hittite, Roman, Ottoman, Austro-Hungarian, British, and Russian empires. All of these empires rose and fell. At their height, they were invincible. But they all declined and eventually disintegrated.

They fell because that is the natural progression of empires which are organic entities of their own. All empires must continually expand. As this becomes more difficult, they bleed the center of the empire so they may keep expanding on their periphery.

Eventually, they reach a point of maximum expansion. Then they begin the process of implosion. They collapse. The process of decline can last hundreds of years, as in the cases of the Ottoman and British empires, or only a few short decades in the case of the largest and most powerful empire the world has ever known, the American empire.

The American empire was born in 1776 from the Revolutionary War with Great Britain. The foundation of the United States of America is based on the sound principles of freedom, rule of law, and representative democracy. The country grew steadily during the 1800s, with the Louisiana Purchase from the French, the Spanish-American War with the Mexicans, and the eventual acquisition of Alaska and Hawaii as the forty-ninth and fiftieth states in the union in 1912.

The American empire went through adolescence in the 1800s, and grew in leaps and bounds, but not without bumps along the way. In the North, slavery had been abolished, but it still continued in the South due to reliance on slaves working on plantations as the major economic engine of the South. This division between the industrial North and the agricultural South almost tore the fledgling empire in two.

According to Wikipedia, "The 1860 election of Abraham Lincoln calling for no more expansion of slavery triggered a crisis as eleven slave states seceded to found the Confederate States of America in 1861. The bloody American Civil War (1861–65) redefined the nation and remains the central iconic event in United States history." (Wikipedia, "History of the United States," http://en.wikipedia.org/wiki/History of the United States (accessed March 22, 2012))

The Confederate South was defeated and slavery was abolished. The secessionist states rejoined the union and the United States withstood the biggest threat to its existence up until that event. Thus, with the wisdom and guidance of President Abraham Lincoln, the American empire survived the Civil War and became more unified than ever.

World War I was the first major role on the global stage for the American empire. It declared war on Germany in 1917 and helped fund the victory of the Allies over the Axis Powers. The Europeans lost millions of lives during World War I, but the United States emerged relatively unscathed. In fact, President Woodrow Wilson formed the League of Nations (the precursor of the United Nations) in 1920 to prevent future global wars. Sadly, the United States did not join the original League of Nations.

The 1920s were a wonderful decade for the United States. But the good times all came crashing down with the stock market crash of 1929, followed by the worldwide Great Depression during the 1930s. This led to a major realignment in American politics, with the election of Franklin D. Roosevelt as president of the United States. Roosevelt created the New Deal, which included major relief and reform for the American people, some of the reforms including the creation of Medicare, Medicaid, and Social Security programs.

The next major shock to the American empire occurred in 1941 with the Japanese attack on Pearl Harbor. The United States cranked up the war machine and entered World War II alongside the Allies. With the U.S.-led invasion of Normandy on "D-Day," the United States helped defeat Nazi Germany in Europe.

Meanwhile, American scientists working on the Manhattan Project raced to create the world's first atomic bomb. The United States dropped the new atomic bombs on Hiroshima and Nagasaki, Japan, in August 1945 and helped defeat Japan, ending World War II.

The United States and the Soviet Union emerged from World War II as superpowers and thus began the Cold War. The superpowers competed with each other in the arms race, the space race, and military interventions in Europe and East Asia. Both superpowers possessed enough nuclear weapons to annihilate one another several times over, so neither was willing to incite a potential nuclear Armageddon. This doctrine was called "MAD" standing for "mutually assured destruction."

The two superpowers ultimately came dangerously close to nuclear war during the Cuban Missile Crisis of 1961, which was brilliantly averted by the deft diplomacy of President John F. Kennedy and of the Soviet Premier, Nikita Khrushchev.

Economically speaking, however, the United States cemented its stature as the world's dominant economic power after World War II. The American GIs returned home from fighting overseas and became the most influential generation in American history, the Baby Boomers. The American economy was the envy of the world.

Meanwhile, the American empire helped rebuild war-torn Europe from the ground up, following the Marshall Plan. It also fought wars in the Philippines, Korea, Vietnam, Iraq, and Afghanistan, and now has military bases and troops in all of those countries. According to the Department of Defense's 2010 Base Structure Report, the U.S. military maintains 662 foreign sites in 38 countries around the world. The United States is a militaristic empire, the largest the world has ever seen. Its military budget of over six hundred billion dollars per year is roughly equal to the rest of the world's military budgets combined.

But in terms of world gross domestic product (GDP), it has seen its share of GDP go from roughly 30 percent of the world's GDP in 1945 to about 22 percent in 2010. (Visualizing Economics, "Share of GDP: China, India, Japan, Latin America, Western Europe, United States," http://visualizingeconomics.com/2008/01/20/share-of-world-gdp (accessed March 22, 2012)) In reality, although some in the United States may believe that they are the world's sole hegemonic power, the reality is that a multipolar world has now formed, with regional powers exerting power in their respective spheres of influence.

President Calvin Coolidge once said, "The business of America is business" (Excerpt from speech in Washington, DC on January 17, 1925, "The Press Under a Free Government"). The American model of business has been exported to the entire world. America was the uncontested leader in many industries including automotive, aeronautic, and health.

Many of the world's greatest discoveries and achievements were made in the United States. For example, Americans won the space race with the Soviet Union when Apollo 11 landed on the moon in 1969. Astronaut Neil Armstrong's words rang out throughout the big blue marble called Earth, "That's one small step for man; one giant leap for mankind."

Henry Ford invented the Model T and became the father of the American automotive industry. General Motors Corporation (GM), the main rival to Ford Motor Company, became the largest corporation in the world. It was said that "what's good for GM is good for America," meaning that the success of GM mirrored the prosperity of the United States (Charles Wilson, Senate Hearing testimony, 1953). Chevrolets were being exported around the world.

More importantly, America was exporting the American business model and the American way of life to the far reaches of the planet. The twentieth century was the American century, and American products like Coca-Cola and Levi's blue jeans were being sold around the world. American movie stars like John Wayne, Humphrey Bogart, and Robert Redford and American pop stars like Elvis Presley and Michael Jackson became world famous, too.

The story of General Motors parallels the overall tale of the American economy rather nicely. GM was founded in Flint, Michigan, in 1908. It grew to be the largest corporation in the world in the 1950s and 1960s. This success is similar to that of the American empire, which became the uncontested world economic powerhouse after World War II.

Under the leadership of Alfred P. Sloan in the 1920s, GM pioneered the management of a complex worldwide organization while developing more and more diverse products as it followed its buyers up the so-called "Ladder of Success." This meant that as the consumer achieved greater success in life, he or she could first buy an entry-level car such as the Chevrolet Cavalier, and could then move up to more and more luxurious vehicles such as the Pontiac, Buick, and Cadillac.

In the early 1950s, GM produced more than 50 percent of all cars and trucks in the United States. GM also exported a large number of cars to countries in the developing world, such as Turkey, because those countries simply did not yet produce automobiles. GM grew and multiplied into several divisions with numerous world famous brands such as Chevrolet, Buick, Cadillac, Pontiac, and Oldsmobile.

With the debut of the 1964 Pontiac GTO, Detroit's powerhouse set about ushering in the era of the muscle car. GM was flexing its muscles and felt invincible. Then the energy crisis of 1978 hit the United States. Suddenly, people didn't want a V-8 engine in a medium sized American body; they wanted a four-cylinder engine in a small sized Japanese body. GM failed to adapt to the changing conditions of the market...as did the American economy at large.

"Manufacturing began moving offshore, as cheaper labor costs drove a competitive wedge between the new Asian producers and the aging, union-saddled companies in the United States. This trend continued

through the 1980s, which saw GM's market share in the United States drop from 45 percent to 35 percent and, for the first time in fifty-nine years, the company actually reported a net loss." (Bowman 2011)

Meanwhile, Japan transformed itself into the miracle economy of the twentieth century. Much has been written about how the Japanese economy became so big and powerful. The Japanese work ethic is one big reason. Japanese firms also seemed to build higher quality products at more affordable prices than did American companies.

Another reason for the Japanese success was innovation in the workplace, such as the just-in-time manufacturing strategy. Postwar Japan perfected the art of reverse engineering American automobiles and electronics, and now dominates both the automotive and electronics industries. Honda, Toyota, and Sony have become household names around the world. The Japanese improved upon our technology and became the second-largest economy in the world until recently being surpassed by China.

In the 1980s, Detroit was shell-shocked by the rapid acceptance of Honda, Toyota, and Nissan vehicles by the American public. The American consumer learned quickly that Japanese cars were, on average, more reliable, cheaper to buy, and more fuel-efficient. The American cars were clumsier and less fuel-efficient.

The combination of fierce competition, high labor costs, and extremely high legacy costs (employee retirement and healthcare costs) eventually forced the once-largest company in the world into bankruptcy in 2009. Not surprisingly, Toyota surpassed General Motors as the world's largest automobile company in 2010.

The American empire was in decline. At the turn of the twenty-first century, it seemed as though the empire was invincible. It had reaped the wealth of the "dot.com revolution" during the 1990s and it seemed like the good times would never end. Then, completely unexpectedly, came the terrorist attacks on the United States on September 11, 2001. This event shook the empire to its core and forced it to rethink the whole myth of the invincible global empire. Americans were shocked and in utter disbelief! "Why would anybody attack us? Is this really happening to us? What did we do to deserve this?"

Americans spent the first decade of the new millennium trying to rid the world of terrorists, while the huge government debt grew ever larger. In April 2011, Standard and Poor's declared that unless serious cuts were made in the annual budget deficit, they would have to downgrade the AAA rating of the United States of America. In August 2011, Standard and Poor's rating agency downgraded the credit rating of the United States for the first time in history. (Washington Post, "S&P downgrades U.S. credit rating for the first time," August 6, 2011. http://www.washingtonpost.com/business/economy/sandp-considering-first-downgrade-of-us-credit-rating/2011/08/05/gIQ (accessed March 13, 2012))

Still, the politicians in power could not agree on how much or what to cut from the federal budget. The American political system was not conducive to politicians making unpopular decisions for the overall benefit of the country. Beginning in 2011, then chairman of the Federal Reserve, Ben Bernanke, started holding regular press conferences declaring that inflation is not a problem, and that he is committed to maintaining a "strong" dollar.

Translation: "We are well aware that inflation is rising rapidly, and we will continue this course until the dollar becomes worthless. We have no other choice except to default on our debt!" Thus, the United States was formally announcing to the world that it was monetizing its debt. This only served to accelerate the demise of the dollar.

This is where the American empire finds itself today—in an irreversible state of rapid decline in which the federal government is desperately trying to pull the wool over the eyes of the American public. The American empire is bankrupt--"the emperor has no clothes," but most Americans still believe the emperor is dressed in his finest regalia.

The American empire appears intact, but it lies directly in the path of a massive dam about to burst. At first, there will be small leaks and cracks in the dam. Then suddenly, the whole dam will collapse, and the empire will be devastated. Those few individuals who see the coming collapse of the dam will move themselves to higher ground. But alas, the vast majority of the empire will be decimated by the flood.

This writing is a desperate call to the few who see the cracks in the dam to take heed immediately. Start building your ark as strongly as possible to weather the coming flood. Do not fear the great flood. Instead, take the necessary precautions, in the last days before the flood, to survive and even thrive during this time of great upheaval.

Those individuals who accurately foresee the imminent demise of the dollar will shift their wealth and savings from dollars to gold, silver, commodities, real estate and other tangible assets. On a broader level, these individuals will take stock of their lives and actively create a more prosperous future for themselves and their loved ones.

For More Information,
Please Visit www.DollarImplosion.com.

CHAPTER 2

DEBT, DEBT AND MORE DEBT

Johnny lived lavishly for many years. Even though he was earning an incredible amount of money through his company, Universal Motors Corporation, his expenses always seemed to be greater than his income. He kept spending more money than he earned.

At first, he used credit cards to merely enhance his life. Then he developed the terrible habit of buying everything with credit cards. It seemed that Johnny had unlimited credit. Everybody just kept lending money to him because they were sure that he could always pay them back.

Nicholas knew deep down inside that Johnny could not possibly pay back all of his debts, so he demanded payment in full of the debt Johnny owed him. Johnny sternly replied to Nicholas, "If you are so bold and strong, than make me pay!" (**France demands payment of its reserves in gold and President Nixon responds by abandoning the Gold Standard in 1971**). *Of course, Nicholas backed down and nobody else dared to make such silly demands of Johnny.*

Johnny bought a huge mansion with seventy-nine rooms and fifty-nine servants in the most expensive neighborhood in town. He bought fast, expensive sports cars and had beautiful mistresses. He threw extravagant parties at his mansion and became known as the wealthiest man in the world. He was on top of the world (**Post-World War II Boom Years**)!

Eventually, Johnny stopped going to the gym and started getting flabby. He gained about seventy-five pounds, but figured he looked better that way. He also found himself drinking alcohol more and more. He wasn't eating as healthy as he used to because he was too busy working and partying. Johnny thought he was living the American Dream.

But his health began to suffer from lack of proper rest and nutrition. At the same time, Johnny's marriage suffered from working long hours. However, Johnny was completely oblivious to the needs of his wife and family. The situation spiraled out of control and led to the dissolution of his marriage (**Saudi Arabia**). Johnny was devastated (**Oil Shocks of 1973 and 1979**)! Johnny's life was out of balance. Was this all a terrible nightmare?

Johnny's financial situation began to deteriorate, as well. He tried to reduce the expenses of the mansion, but with only limited success. He fired twenty-five servants and had to make do with only thirty-four servants! He even thought about selling his 159-ft mega yacht, "American Dream," but he could not bear the thought of letting it go. Johnny simply could not give up his extravagant lifestyle. He had grown accustomed to partying until the wee hours of the morning and could not bring himself to lead a boring and unexciting life.

Johnny's storybook life had definitely taken a turn for the worse. Between the banks and the lawyers, Johnny's good credit and assets were destroyed and he was left heavily in debt, with almost no possibility of ever getting out of it. All this debt was held by the banks (**International Banking Cartel**) and they could destroy his life any time they might choose to. Johnny's American Dream had become a nightmare. Johnny was no longer invincible.

One principal tenet of the American empire is, "Banks always win." They won again in October 2008, when the United States government bailed out the banks with the "TARP" (Troubled Asset Relief Program) to the tune of $787 billion. This is why the little guy needs support against large institutions like banks and corporations...because the little guy loses every time.

This sentiment—"the little guy loses every time"—was recently brought to the forefront of American political discourse with the rise of the Occupy Wall Street movement. The Occupy movement is an international protest movement which seeks to change the structure of contemporary society to a more equitable one that benefits the vast majority of people rather than the privileged few. Hence the slogan of the movement, **"We are the 99%."**

This movement arguably began on September 17, 2011 with the "occupation" of Zuccotti Park in New York City by an ardent group of protesters. By early October 2011, the Occupy protests were ongoing in over 95 cities across 82 countries and over 600 communities in the United States. (Wikipedia, "Occupy movement," http://en.wikipedia.org/wiki/Occupy_movement (accessed March 14, 2012))

The movement was inspired by the events of the "Arab Spring" earlier that year in which protesters in Cairo, Egypt occupied the central, Tahrir Square until their demand that Hosni Mubarak, the Egyptian dictator, step down was met. In just a few short months, with minimal bloodshed, Mubarak relinquished his post as the Egyptian dictator. The Occupy movement was also influenced by the anti-austerity protests in Greece and Spain in 2010-11.

The allegorical Johnny didn't realize it, but he was actually going through the grieving process during his long, painful divorce. Initially, he was in denial, which is the first stage of the Kubler-Ross

Model of grief, developed by Elisabeth Kubler-Ross in her 1969 book, *On Death and Dying*.

In her landmark book, Kubler-Ross describes the five stages of the grieving process:

(1) Denial: "This can't be happening to me!"
(2) Anger: "It's all his fault."
(3) Bargaining: "Please God, I will do anything for another chance."
(4) Depression: "What's the point of trying? I'm going to die anyway."
(5) Acceptance: "I might as well accept my fate."

Originally, Kubler-Ross applied these stages to people suffering from terminal illness. Later she applied this model to any form of catastrophic personal loss such as death of a loved one, a divorce, a debilitating accident, and other major life events.

Kubler-Ross claimed that these steps do not necessarily come in the order noted above, nor are all steps experienced by all patients, though she stated that a person will always experience at least two. Often people will experience several stages in a "roller coaster" effect—switching between two or more stages, returning to one or more several times before working through it.

Similarly, the United States of America is going bankrupt and experiencing the Kubler-Ross grieving process on a grand scale. Bankruptcy for the American empire became reality with the great "Bubblequake" of 2008. Since then, Americans have been experiencing denial, anger, and bargaining both individually and collectively. "The United States of America, the greatest nation on earth, could not possibly be going bankrupt!" "It's all the rotten politicians' fault." "If we just get our economic house in order, everything will work out fine." These are some of the outward expressions of denial and anger we hear today.

Next, the American empire will experience depression and,

finally, acceptance. The economic depression of the United States will last at least until 2023. It will be akin to the Great Depression of the 1930s and will become a global economic depression. Finally, the American empire and the entire planet will accept the limitations of bankruptcy and will evolve into an economically and socially integrated planetary consciousness based on individual empowerment.

PARALLEL EVOLUTION OF MONEY AND DEBT

Money is defined by Merriam-Webster's Online Dictionary (http://www.merriam-webster.com/dictionary/money, (accessed 3/13/2012)) as a "standard of value, store of value, and a medium of exchange." Human beings have used many different forms of money including seashells, tea, and livestock. But these items were perishable and not very durable. Then humans used bronze, copper, silver, and gold as the primary forms of money.

James Turk and John Rubino give an excellent synopsis of the rise of fiat currencies in the West in *The Collapse of the Dollar and How to Profit from It* (2004). They describe how the first true gold coins were found in Lydia, in present-day Turkey, around 600 B.C. Since then, just about every civilization, large and small, has used metal coins as money.

Gold became synonymous with wealth and power. As the European civilizations grew and expanded, they conquered and pillaged the new world in search of fabled cities of gold, such as "El Dorado," a search that paved the way for the colonization of the new world by Europeans.

In the 1690s, the Bank of England had a stroke of genius and started issuing paper "pounds," in place of circulating gold and silver coins. This was a conceptual breakthrough. The paper pound became the first widely circulated paper currency in the world. This served the British Empire well for over two hundred years. This paper currency was linked to the value of the gold held by the Bank of England. This arrangement became known as the "classical gold standard."

In the 1770s, the Continental Congress of the United States began printing its own currency, Continentals, to finance the Revolutionary War. But this currency failed, as the currency had no solid backing of gold. In 1793, the United States began minting gold and silver coins. In the early 1800s, the country created the Bank of the United States and the Second Bank of the United States, which performed early central bank functions.

In 1828, President Andrew Jackson ushered in the "Free Banking Era," declaring that any bank could print its own currency, as long as it was backed by gold. Dozens of currencies were circulating in various parts of the United States. But this interesting experiment ended with the start of the Civil War. President Lincoln signed the National Banking Act of 1863, creating the national currency known as the "greenback."

In the post-Civil War years, the United States used a bimetallic system based on silver and gold. Then in 1900, the United States joined Britain, Germany and most other countries by adopting the monometallic system based on gold. During the 1900s, actual gold would be transported from countries running deficits to the countries to which they owed money.

But the bankers became greedy again, and devised the fractional reserve system in which they only kept a fraction of the currency they issued, typically 10 percent. Fractional reserve banking became the norm, and this system functioned quite well. The result was a "flexible" money supply which expanded to meet the growing needs of the global economy. Because it was backed by gold, inflation was virtually nonexistent. Capital flowed freely from country to country, trade barriers were inconsequential, and global economic activity was robust. (Turk and Rubino 2004, 54–55)

But the size of government in the United States and abroad kept growing. In 1883, German chancellor Otto von Bismarck created the first welfare state by instituting mandatory national health insurance, social insurance, accident insurance, and unemployment insurance. Most of Europe and Russia followed suit. Meanwhile, the U.S. government tightened its hold on its financial system by creating the Federal Reserve in 1913. People's desire for an expanding safety net around the world was a major step forward for humanity. The modern welfare state had become firmly established in the West by the mid twentieth century.

Then, Europe burst into flames in 1914 with the assassination of Archduke Ferdinand of Austria-Hungary by a Serbian gunman. The governments of Europe again cranked up the printing presses and severed their links to gold. Only the United States stayed on the gold standard.

Newly awash in all the dollars printed during World War I, "the stock market and real estate markets boomed as the masses discovered the joys of speculating with borrowed funds." (Turk and Rubino 2004, 58) Then the stock market crashed in 1929. Thus began the Great Depression, which lasted about ten years. The major governments of the world responded by creating tariffs and trade barriers and by devaluing their currencies. The Western industrialized world was going through growing pains it could not have imagined at the turn of the twentieth century.

In the United States, Americans started cashing in their dollars for gold, in droves. The fractional reserve banking system was thrown in reverse. United States' banks failed by the thousands. Businesses could not get credit and failed. Newly unemployed workers spent less money, and prices went down further in a vicious cycle. President Franklin D. Roosevelt responded by taking the dollar off the gold standard and began the confiscation of privately held gold by issuing an executive order:

> *I, Franklin D. Roosevelt, President of the United States of America…do hereby prohibit the hoarding of gold coin, gold bullion, and gold certificates within the continental United States.*
>
> *All persons are hereby required to deliver on or before May 1, 1933, to a Federal Reserve bank or a branch or agency thereof or to any member bank of the Federal Reserve System all gold coin, gold bullion, and gold certificates now owned by them or coming into their ownership on or before April 28, 1933.*

Whoever willfully violates any provision of this Executive Order may be fined not more than $10,000, or imprisoned for not more than ten years or both (President Franklin Roosevelt, Executive Order 6102, April 5, 1933)

Once the United States government completed the process of confiscating the gold of its citizens for $20.67 an ounce, the Treasury devalued the dollar to $35 an ounce in 1934. History then dealt another blow to the West with the rise of Adolph Hitler and World War II. Tens of millions of lives were lost on all sides. The American empire flexed her muscles and triumphed over the Axis Powers of Germany, Italy and Japan.

Essentially, the mighty American empire delivered Europe from the hands of a ruthless dictator to freedom and democracy. The Marshall Plan was devised to rebuild Europe to help it once again become the economic powerhouse that now rivals the United States. The victors of World War II met in Bretton Woods, New Hampshire, in 1944, and essentially made the U.S. dollar the world's reserve currency.

The 1950s were the golden years of the American empire. A huge new generation of Americans, the Baby Boomers, was born between 1946 and 1964. These Baby Boomers would change the world forever. But America also fought the Korean War in the 1950s and the Vietnam War in the 1960s to contain the Soviet Union during the ongoing, larger Cold War.

At the same time, the U.S. government created the "Great Society" welfare programs such as Medicare and Social Security. As a result, the country had to print more money and go further into debt to finance these wars as well as the needs of the growing welfare state.

This increase in the circulating dollars led to a rapid increase in demand for gold, as dollars became less valuable. The French called the American empire's bluff in 1970, by cashing in their U.S. dollars for gold. They knew the United States simply did not possess enough gold to back its currency. In 1971, President Nixon officially took the United States off the gold standard and the rest of the world followed suit. As a result, governments and central banks of each country could print their currency according to the prevailing politics of the day. But of course, this naturally led to larger and larger government debt in the United States and abroad.

This arrangement worked well until the devastating first oil shock of 1973 and the second oil shock of 1978. The value of the dollar plunged, inflation and unemployment went into the double digits, and gold rose to over eight hundred dollars an ounce. Thus began the inexorable loss of value of the dollar versus gold.

Since the 1970s, the U.S. government has actively engaged in blowing economic bubbles. It had to create economic bubbles because the productivity of the United States had peaked at about 0.6 percent per year in 1970. In 2011, U.S. productivity was still growing at about 0.6 percent per year.

So the U.S. government has chosen to keep the party going by creating and expanding the massive real estate, stock market, and private equity bubbles. It did this by keeping interest rates near zero, thereby providing massive liquidity to the financial markets. The financial markets, in turn, lent this money freely to the American public, who purchased real estate and stocks and bought tons of merchandise on credit.

Not surprisingly, these bubbles popped in the great economic downturn of late 2008. They will pop further when the largest two bubbles, the dollar bubble and the government debt bubble pop later this decade and early next decade. Then the whole American bubble economy will be deflated, which will trigger a global economic depression. Once deflated, economic bubbles do not re-inflate; they stay deflated until the underlying fundamentals of the economy become stronger.

Until the 1980s, U.S. debt and gross domestic product (GDP) rose in tandem, which meant that our economic growth supported the increasing amounts of government debt. However, around 1985, the per capita debt began growing much faster than per capita GDP. In fact, while per capita GDP has grown to a respectable $40,000, per capita debt rose to approximately $150,000 in the same time period! (Turk and Rubino 2004, ix–x)

By the turn of the millennium, this became the portrait of the United States: *a people living far beyond their means and headed for disaster*. In late 2011, U.S. national debt exceeded $15 trillion-- roughly one hundred percent of the United States annual GDP. In 2018, the U.S. national debt is roughly $22 trillion and increasing by over $1 trillion each and every year.

At the same time, the United States' annual budget deficit in 2011 was approximately $1.5 trillion, due to fighting two simultaneous wars, due to massive government bailouts of the major banks, insurance companies, Fannie Mae, Freddie Mac, and GM and Chrysler, and due to the massive federal government stimulus plan. In fact, even the most conservative forecasters predict ever-increasing deficits throughout the decade.

The problem is that it is very difficult to shrink the deficit. In fact, since the 1960s, the United States has been running structural deficits. A structural deficit is a permanent, built-in deficit due to recurring government expenditures such as Medicare/Medicaid, Social Security, and Defense. President Clinton's administration actually ran surpluses in the late 1990s, but Americans reverted to their old ways of huge $400 to $500 billion deficits during the President George W. Bush years. Like a junkie, America has become addicted to spending beyond its means.

American cities and states are now going bankrupt. However, unlike the federal government, city and state governments cannot simply loan themselves more money out of thin air. Only the federal government can print currency, according to the Constitution. So the cities and states of the United States must adjust to the new reality, while the federal government in Washington, D.C. continues to live beyond its means.

No politician dares cut the bulk (over 60 percent) of government spending that goes to Medicare, Social Security, and Defense. The rest of the government's "discretionary" spending goes to education, infrastructure, and social programs. It is nearly impossible for American politicians to run on platforms of cutting government programs or raising taxes. They simply don't stand a chance to get elected on those platforms. They can't even cut a sizable fraction of the deficit such as $100 billion. So Americans now live with a sea of red ink as far as the eye can see with no end in sight!

Adam Smith's "invisible hand" of the market eventually takes care of the imbalances in the world's economies, as Americans learned in late 2008. First, Bear Stearns, an investment bank, tanked, and nobody could save it. Then Lehman Brothers, another investment bank, went under. Then AIG, one of the largest insurance companies in the world, was about to go under until the U.S. government stepped in and bailed it out with $180 billion of taxpayer money. The major U.S. banks saw their stock plummet. Even the U.S. automakers, GM, Ford, and Chrysler, were in trouble.

In late 2008, all the politicians and pundits said that the whole U.S. economy and maybe even the global economy would collapse if the U.S. government did not step in and bail out the banks, insurance companies, Fannie Mae and Freddie Mac, and the auto companies. The U.S. government spent extraordinary amounts of money bailing out these institutions—over $12 trillion. (Wiedemer et al. 2010, 79)

Specifically, the U.S. government spent $7.7 trillion on direct investments in financial institutions, corporate debt, and mortgage-backed securities, $2.3 trillion on lending to banks, and $2.1 trillion on government insurance of bank and Fannie Mae and Freddie Mac assets. This dramatically increased the overall money supply to over $1600 trillion! (Wiedemer et al. 2010, 78)

So does the U.S. government have a credit limit? When will the largest and last two great bubbles pop? Many experts predict that this will occur when foreign lenders dramatically reduce the amount of lending to the United States because they are concerned about being repaid in dollars that have less value than the dollars they are lending.

The World Bank estimates that our national credit limit is $25 trillion. In 2012, the United States' national debt exceeded $15 trillion and the country was accumulating more debt at the rate of

$1.5 to $2 trillion per year. In late 2015, that number was nearly $19 trillion, but the nation was accumulating the debt at a slightly slower rate of $1 trillion per year. At this rate, the United States government will certainly reach or exceed its credit limit of $25 trillion by 2023. At that point, the United States government will have reached its credit limit and will be forced to default on its debt payments.

As of December 2010, the national unemployment rate stood at 9.8 percent. In 2015, the federal government claims that the unemployment is between 5 and 6 percent. However, the government does not count those who are discouraged-unemployed or underemployed. If the statisticians counted those folks, the unemployment figure would be around 23 percent, according to John Williams' ShadowStats.com.

The United States is headed for double-digit inflation because of the rate at which the broader money supply is increasing. It simply takes six to eighteen months to for this to happen. The M1 money supply (amount of money in circulation) increased 15 percent during the government bailouts of late 2008 to early 2009. (Wiedemer et al. 2010, 83)

But will the government keep increasing the money supply? The answer is a resounding "Yes!" The continued housing market collapse, commercial real estate market collapse, and high unemployment, combined with the government's inability to spend within its means, requires it to continue the upward spiral of increasing money supply.

Double-digit inflation inevitably leads to double-digit interest rates. Otherwise, nobody will lend the United States money. So interest rates are sure to rise in the next few years. This is when it gets interesting. The government will be forced to raise interest rates to entice investors to keep investing in the languishing U.S. economy.

At first, it may seem a temporary measure to "cool down" the economy. But soon the American people will realize that this is no ordinary rise in interest rates. It will seem like there is no end to the constant increase in prices of goods and services along with the rising interest rates. The United States will be living its own version of the Weimar Republic! Inflation may become so terrible that the American public actually welcomes a new currency.

However, a new currency will be only a temporary solution. What is truly needed to make America solvent again will be structural changes in its economy and drastic cuts in government services. When the United States no longer runs trillion dollar deficits, it will be strong and competitive once again. Knowing the nature of politics in the United States, it will be quite difficult and will require steadfast resolve on the part of the entire electorate to accomplish this feat.

THE SQUEEZE ON STATE AND LOCAL GOVERNMENTS

Beginning in 2010, governors of many U.S. states were being forced to cut their budgets and raise taxes to cope with their budget shortfalls. Collectively, state governments were in the hole in the amount of some $500 billion. Many governors and state legislators, who were overwhelmingly Republican, were swept into office in a wave of anti-incumbent sentiment in 2010 that seems to have mandated cutting state and federal government budget deficits. Americans figured, "I have to live according to a budget; so should the government!"

Interestingly, many governors and state legislators have interpreted the mandate to mean cutting the budget by whatever means possible, including rescinding the rights of government workers. The governor of Wisconsin went so far as trying to pass a bill that takes away the right of government workers to bargain collectively. The middle-class workers of Wisconsin were in danger of losing some of the hard-fought rights of the working class. Similar battles were raging on in Ohio, Indiana, and Michigan.

The middle class in the United States has been losing ground since 1970. Real wages have been stagnant for over forty years. The middle class has been borrowing just to maintain its standard of living. Now state governments are starting to squeeze the working and middle classes in a very real way by cutting pensions, healthcare benefits, and wages, and by simultaneously attempting to bust the unions.

One of the hallmarks of a great civilization is the creation of a large, vibrant middle class. After World War II, the United States built the largest middle class in history. The mortgage system was utilized to buy homes and leases were used to buy cars. Everything could be bought on credit and the economy boomed. The American consumer economy became the largest market in the world. The American consumer had developed a voracious appetite that seemed to have no limit. Americans bought everything from flat-screen TVs to computers to expensive cars. The good times were rolling, or so it seemed.

However, in the 1980s, both personal and government debt grew out of proportion to the growth of the economy. The average savings rate for Americans actually became negative by 2000. It continued on this trajectory as consumers began borrowing against the value of their homes in the real estate bubble of the 2000s. According to George Soros, the billionaire investor who made billions from the collapse of the British pound in 1992, this debt bubble is the "Super Bubble." The Super Bubble arose from globalization and from the incredible flow of capital into the United States, starting in the 1980s.

Developing countries had to play by the rules laid out by the International Monetary Fund and the World Bank. However, the United States did not have to play by those rules and abused its privilege of having the world's reserve currency. Both the public and private sector in the United States began to live beyond their means, and they still continue on this trajectory today.

This early period of globalization was a great time for the United States. Many developing nations began to join the global economy. Due to lower labor costs in those countries, goods and services began to be outsourced to nations outside the United States. The United States, naturally being the largest consumer market in the world, bought up the cheaper goods and services from abroad. The sellers of the cheaper goods, such as the Japanese and Chinese, turned around and bought U.S. bonds and Treasuries to help keep U.S. interest rates low. In effect, these countries funded the U.S. trade and budget deficits. So the United States kept on printing dollars without a corresponding rise in inflation.

Unfortunately, the party could not last forever. During the early 2000s, private debt began to explode. Alan Greenspan, Chairman of the Federal Reserve during the fallout from the bursting of the tech bubble in 2000 and the subsequent terrorist attacks on the twin towers on 9/11, cut interest rates to 1 percent and kept the party going. This easy money added fuel to the fire by continuing to expand the housing, private equity, and debt bubbles. The party ended in late 2008 with the collapse of the sub-prime mortgage market, investment banks, and the housing market. American consumers could no longer borrow against the value of their homes to buy more stuff from foreigners, and foreigners had less money to pump back into the U.S. economy. America's Super Bubble had burst and Americans could no longer afford to live beyond their means.

Still, the United States government continues to live beyond its means. When the U.S. dollar begins to implode later this decade, the United States government will get its first real wake-up call. Things will then go from bad to worse for the American empire and there will be no easy solution to the problems it faces. Going bankrupt is not easy for individuals, corporations or for governments. But this is precisely what the American empire is going through at this stage of history. After experiencing the "worst economic depression in history," it will probably take several more years before the federal government is finally forced to live according to its means.

For More Information,
Please Visit www.DollarImplosion.com.

CHAPTER 3

CHINESE DRAGON AWAKENS

*Around the same time that Johnny became middle-aged, numerous other young men were coming of age in neighboring towns. A young man named Hiroto (**Japan**) was determined to build the world's largest automobile company. Hiroto had become adept at copying and improving upon Johnny's success. He studied Johnny's automobiles and improved on the components and systems. This process was called reverse engineering and Hiroto became an expert at it.*

At first, everybody laughed at Hiroto's cheap imitation automobiles. With intense determination and a strong work ethic, however, his cars became better and better. He built his own automobile factory and called it Hirohito Motors Corporation. Hiroto strove to build cars that were more fuel-efficient, more reliable, and more affordable than Johnny's. Hiroto eventually succeeded and he did so in a relatively short period of time. Johnny was seriously challenged by the success of Hiroto's business model. In fact, Hiroto grew to be the second-richest man in the neighborhood next to Johnny.

*Minjoon (**South Korea**) heard about Johnny and Hiroto's success and he started building cars, too. He called his company Sundai Motors. At first, everybody laughed at him as well. How could he compete with Johnny and Hiroto? Minjoon's new cars just didn't have the horsepower and were not particularly elegant in design.*

But over a few short years and after lots of hard work, Minjoon began producing cars that were not only as powerful as Johnny and Hiroto's cars, but they were also less expensive, more fuel-efficient and more sleek in design. Minjoon's cars were winning all kinds of awards including "Car of the Year." Minjoon became a true player in the automobile manufacturing game. Johnny was no longer the only game in town. He had to share the automobile market with Hiroto, Minjoon, Karl, Oliver and others.

Meanwhile, another young man named Chen (**China**) from a distant neighborhood was busy studying the methods of Johnny and Hiroto. Chen built his own automobile factory and began churning out affordable small cars. At first, Chen's cars left a lot to be desired. Then he developed a manufacturing innovation which would propel him to the top of the manufacturing world.

Chen took the concept of reverse engineering and applied it to each individual step of the manufacturing process. He began to improve upon the individual components of the car, rather than simply copy Johnny's and Hiroto's cars precisely. Chen was able to build cars that were even more affordable, fuel-efficient, and reliable than Hiroto's or Minjoon's. He became a major player in the automobile manufacturing game. Chen applied his manufacturing model to almost every product imaginable. In fact, Chen became so good at producing low-cost products that he became the factory to the entire neighborhood. Johnny's factories began closing their doors because they simply could not compete with Chen's cheaper products.

Johnny was earning less, spending more and going deeper and deeper into debt. After his costly and contentious divorce, Johnny just didn't have the same resources or strength. Interestingly, though, Johnny's biggest creditors were Hiroto and Chen. They kept on loaning money to Johnny because they believed that Johnny could eventually pay it back. After all, they owed much of their success to Johnny. They had simply emulated and improved upon Johnny's success.

Now Johnny, Hiroto, and Chen were all dependent upon each other. Nobody wanted to see anybody else go bankrupt because that would *negatively affect everybody else. It was a wonderful system: Hiroto, Chen, Minjoon and others produced and sold products to Johnny, who bought the products with money he didn't have, putting Johnny deeper and deeper into debt. The effects of this structural imbalance between Johnny and his peers would soon wreak havoc on the entire neighborhood.*

China now boasts the nation with the largest number of Internet users in the world, with 457 million users at the end of 2010, according to a report from the China Internet Network Information Center. That's more than one-third of the Asian giant's population and 73 million more people than in 2009. One cannot underestimate the profound impact of the Internet on the world's geopolitical power structure.

Furthermore, the Chinese are starting to invest their huge surpluses in businesses, resources, and countries around the world. Australia, Africa and South America are seeing a tremendous amount of Chinese investment in natural resource companies and infrastructure. China's appetite for raw materials seems insatiable and they are quickly buying up the companies that procure those natural resources.

China has become the world's largest market for automobiles and boasts the largest number of Internet users in the world. When Deng Xiaoping was telling the Chinese masses that "to get rich is glorious," Americans—and their European cousins—were beginning to spend more than they earned, relying on debt to finance their increasingly extravagant lifestyles, rather than on savings and capital formation. (Orville Schell, "To Get Rich Is Glorious: China in the 80's," 1984)

The world is witnessing the rise of China again, which actually surpassed Japan as the world's second-largest economy in 2010 and is now *the* major competitor to the United States. China is booming! It has become the factory to the world. As a result, the Chinese now possess the largest amount of U.S. Treasury bonds in the world— worth over one trillion dollars. (United States Treasury, "Major Foreign Holders of Treasury Securities," http://www.treasury.gov/ resource-center/data-chart-center/tic/Documents/mfh.txt (accessed March 22, 2012))

China will definitely play the pivotal role in the downfall of the American empire, simply because it is now the world's second largest economy and poised to rival the United States. It seems global economic growth and wealth is shifting from the rich, industrialized West to the rapidly developing nations of the East with China at the forefront of this trend.

It is common knowledge that China is the world's most populous country with a population of 1.35 billion people. We Americans also now know that China's nominal GDP in 2015 is estimated to be $11.212 trillion which is the 2nd largest in the world behind the United States. However, it may not be so widely known that the Purchasing Power Parity (PPP) GDP of China in 2015 is estimated at $18.976 trillion which is the largest in the world!

Chinese history dates back to the Xia dynasty which emerged around 2100 BCE. The succeeding Shang dynasty is the earliest to be confirmed by contemporary records and ruled the Yellow River plain from the 17th to the 11th century BCE. Subsequent ruling dynasties include the Zhou, Qin, Han, Jin, Sui, Tang, Song, Yuan, Ming, and finally the Qing dynasty which lasted from 1644 until 1912. The Republic of China lasted from 1912 to 1949. The Chinese Civil War ended in 1949 with the Communist Party gaining control of most of mainland China and forming the People's Republic of China that exists today.

China is the second-largest country in the world by land area after Russia and has the longest combined land border in the world, measuring 22,117 km or 13,743 miles from the mouth of the Yalu River to the Gulf of Tonkin. China borders 14 nations, more than any other country except Russia, which also borders 14. These bordering countries include Vietnam, Laos and Myanmar in Southeast Asia, India, Bhutan, Nepal and Pakistan in South Asia, Afghanistan, Tajikistan, Kyrgyzstan and Kazakhstan in Central Asia, and Russia, Mongolia, and North Korea in Inner and Northeast Asia. Additionally, China shares maritime boundaries with South Korea, Japan, Vietnam and the Philippines. (Wikipedia, "China," https://en.wikipedia.org/wiki/China (accessed September 24, 2015))

Suffice to say that China is now a formidable competitor to the United States in nearly every way imaginable. The Chinese economy continues to grow at around 7% per year while the United States economy is reportedly growing at roughly 2% per year (many analysts actually believe the United States economy is stagnant or actually contracting, but that is another discussion). Thus, it is clear that China leads the charge of the developing world for achieving higher and higher standards of living and overall wealth akin to that of the Western industrialized world.

In his recent book titled, *The Death of Money*, James Rickards discusses how the international monetary system has collapsed three times in the past hundred years—in 1914, 1939, and 1971—and that we are currently in the throes of the next collapse. Mr. Rickards points out that the biggest economic competitors to the United States--China, Russia and the oil-producing nations of the Middle East--are doing everything possible to end U.S. monetary hegemony.

China, in particular, has been engaging in a concerted effort to drastically increase its gold holdings as a hedge against the collapse of the dollar. Mr. Rickards states that China has increased its domestic gold holdings, both public and private, by approximately 4,500 tons since the last official update of its central bank reserves in 2009. If half of this amount, 2,250 tons, is added to the official reserves figure of 1,054 tons, then China has roughly 3,300 tons of gold as of 2013. If it adds another 700 tons to its reserves throughout 2014, total Chinese reserves would be 4,000 tons by early 2015.

With 4,000 tons, China will surpass France, Italy, Germany and the IMF in the ranks of the world's largest gold holders, and it will be second only to the United States. This would be in keeping with China's status as the world's second-largest economy (The Death of Money, Rickards, 2014, 228-9).

In August 2015, the IMF confirmed that inclusion of the Chinese yuan in the IMF's basket of currencies, the SDR, would be put off for at least a year. So China decided to take matters into its own hands by rapidly devaluing its currency by 2% in two weeks and selling off $100 billion of US Treasuries. With the concurrent drop in the Chinese stock market and real estate market, the Chinese can say that they are taking these steps to prop up the stock market and to sustain their export market which will help the average Chinese citizen.

On top of these moves in August 2015, China did something

even more bold which was confirmed by Bloomberg after being reported by Zerohedge earlier in August 2015. China made the stunning change in the accounting of their gold reserves by deciding to mark their central bank-held gold reserves to market. The "gold" at Fort Knox is not marked to market, it is "fixed" by the Federal Reserve and the U.S. Treasury and is not open to public scrutiny. This kind of "fixing" of the U.S. gold reserves and the "fixing" of the price of gold itself by New York and London will have no part in the new global financial system spearheaded by China (The Wealth Watchman, accessed September 3, 2015).

The map below shows all the countries that have opened up their gold reserves to be marked "to market" in green:

Nearly all of Eurasia is green in the map! According to the Wealth Watchman, this means the following: "It means that the Eurasian bloc is pro-gold and that they intend for gold to have a future as a top-tier, reserve asset on their books, and likely, within their trade as well. It means China, Russia, India and Europe will be setting the new rules for the new system, not the New York and London tag-team, and that this new system will be based on a better international anchor, to determine real value for everyone. . ."

"The only way that gold (and silver) can be used, en masse, again, to settle trade between nations or individuals, is by treating them as special, top tier assets. . .and then by allowing those assets to freely float against the currencies of the world." (The Wealth Watchman, "Beijing Just Buried its Fangs into the US Dollar Standard," http://thewealthwatchman.com/beijing-just-buried-its-fangs-into-the-us-dollar-standard/ (accessed September 11, 2015))

China, Russia and much of the international community are signaling that they are ready to discard the current U.S. dollar standard and embrace the "***return of the gold standard***" as the anchor of the international monetary system. A small but growing number of Americans and Europeans, especially the wealthy, are also preparing for the coming "return of the gold standard" by converting their assets into gold, silver, land, and artwork—those tangible things that will retain their value once the dollar implodes.

How will the Gold Standard return as the foundation of the international monetary system? Dr. Jim Willie, author of the Hat Trick Letter at www.goldenjackass.com, has proposed the most likely scenario of how this will take place. He has made it his passion to carefully and methodically analyze the demise of the dollar as the world's reserve currency. His arguments are sound and his predictions are highly accurate. Here is a synopsis of Dr. Willie's thesis of how the Dollar Standard will be replaced by the Gold Standard in the next few years.

In August 2015, the IMF refused to include the Chinese Renminbi (RMB) in their currency basket. In response, China began to hasten its efforts to dislocate the US dollar from its perch in trade and banking. The immediate response was to devalue Chinese RMB by 2% and sell off $100 billion in US Treasuries in two weeks. But Dr. Willie asserts that the Chinese will exert "extreme pressures to accelerate the increasing required usage of Chinese RMB in trade settlement. These pressures to use RMB in trade include:

1) **The creation of widespread usage of RMB Swap Facilities for bilateral trade between nations with China.**
2) **The coercion of the Saudis to accept RMB currency for oil shipments, the flashpoint that leads to all of the Gulf Emirate nations accepting RMB.**
3) **The eventual refusal by Eastern manufacturing nations to accept US Treasury Bills as payment for goods.**

The first pressure has already been in place for nearly a decade. The second pressure is soon to come as evidenced by the dismantling of the petrodollar and the "divorce" between the United States and Saudi Arabia. Saudi Arabia's new suitor is China since China has now surpassed the United States as the largest purchaser of Saudi oil.

The third pressure will be the "straw that broke the camel's back." This is the trump card that the Chinese have yet to play. It will be the checkmate move by the Chinese vis-à-vis the United States because the United States has become so dependent on Chinese manufactured goods to keep its economy running smoothly.

Once the above-mentioned conditions are met, i.e. Chinese government bonds become widely purchased around the globe, Gulf nations accept RMB for oil payment from China and other Eastern countries, and the RMB becomes widely used in trade settlement, Dr. Willie believes that the "grand dump of US Treasuries from Eastern banking systems will begin." This will be followed by essentially the entire world diversifying out of US Bonds in their banking systems.

When the tsunami of US Treasuries and Bonds washes up on the shores of the United States, the US Federal Reserve and US Treasury Department will have to launch a new "gold-based" Treasury Dollar which Dr. Willie calls the "Scheiss Dollar" because of its phony gold foundation. Dr. Willie emphatically states that there will be an initial 30% devaluation of this currency followed by another 30% devaluation resulting in a 50% devaluation of this New Treasury Dollar. Then comes import price inflation, supply shortages and civil disorder.

Dr. Willie predicts that the new Scheiss Dollar will be one of a parade of new gold-backed currencies around the world. However, the Scheiss Dollar will fail foreign scrutiny because Dr. Willie asserts that the United States does not actually possess the 8,133 tons of gold which it claims to have. Dr. Willie believes it has all been sold by previous administrations unbeknownst to the American public. As a result, the United States finds itself on the slippery slope of becoming a Third World country, states Dr. Willie.

In the brave new world of the Scheiss Dollar and gold-backed currencies of the all major countries, gold will find its true value at **$10,000 per ounce** and silver will find its true value at over **$400 per ounce**, predicts Dr. Willie. Thus, the historic gold-to-silver ratio of 25-to-1 will be preserved. These values for the precious metals will be reached by a progression of steps or quantum leaps. Dr. Willie puts it this way, "The major upcoming events will be exciting to watch unfold, one after the other, in an inevitable sequence away from fascism and concentrated unipolar power, with a strong movement toward freedom and equitable systems with distributed power. . .The steps involve:

1) The critical mass of rejected US T-Bills in trade settlement, citing its corrupt roots and illicit monetary policy as foundation
2) The return to the Gold Trade Standard and introduction of Gold Trade Notes as letters of credit, in replacement for a fair tangible payment system (no more IOU coupons)
3) The recapitalization of the global banking system with Gold as primary reserve asset, so as to relieve the grotesque stagnation, insolvency, and dysfunction [of the current economic system]
4) The seeking of equilibrium in Supply vs. Demand in the new fair uninhibited market, with exclusive control removed from London and New York, and place elsewhere like Shanghai, Hong Kong, Dubai and Singapore
5) The seeding of BRICS gold and silver backed currencies from participating nations within the Alliance (likely several with slight variation in features)
6) The re-opening of the gold mine industry with some blue sky, and relief from the Evergreen element at Barrick
7) The remedy toward owners of over 40,000 tons of re-hypothecated and stolen gold in bullion banks across the world (primarily in Switzerland)

There you have it! This is the most likely scenario of how the US Dollar will be replaced by gold as the world's reserve currency—**the Return of the Gold Standard**. This entire process of dollar implosion followed by return of the gold standard begins in late 2015 and will likely be completed by 2023. This period of eight years, 2015 to 2023, promises to be a tumultuous time—a time of both crisis and opportunity as the Chinese are fond of saying. The dollar will lose its reserve currency status and the fascist business model will give way to a more equitable economic system for all, not just for the privileged few.

The dollar implosion and subsequent return of the gold standard cannot be stopped. This is the natural evolution of the global economy. It is better to understand and see the big picture of what is happening on the global stage. Once we understand the process, we can begin to take the necessary steps to survive and even prosper during this time of structural change in our economy and in our worldview—a paradigm shift from the deterministic, mechanistic top-down Industrial Age to the creative, bottom-up **Age of the Individual**.

For More Information,
Please Visit www.DollarImplosion.com.

ACT II

COLLAPSE OF THE DOLLAR AND THE WORLD ECONOMIC SYSTEM

CHAPTER 4

COLLAPSE OF DICTATORSHIPS AROUND THE WORLD

In late January 2011, a young man named Mohammed rebelled against the village chieftain in Tunisia and drove the chieftain out of town (**Birth of the Arab Awakening**). Everybody in town was shocked, not only by what had happened, but also because they simply did not realize the extent to which Mohammed and his siblings were being exploited by the dictatorial chieftain.

In a nearby town, a young man named Hassan heard about Mohammed's rebellion against the village chieftain. His village chieftain, Hosni, was even more ruthless than Mohammed's. So he challenged the chieftain, Hosni, to a duel one hot summer day.

The sweat began to bead on their foreheads. They looked each other in the eye for what seemed like an eternity. But Hosni could not bear to inflict harm on a member of his own tribe, so he backed down and let Hassan take over the family business (**Hosni Mubarak steps down as dictator of Egypt**).

Hassan became the new village chieftain and distributed the wealth equitably among all the members of his clan. Hassan celebrated his victory against the chieftain by dancing in the street and all of the townspeople filled the streets and rejoiced, "Hassan is free!" Hassan had emerged victorious in his crusade for economic opportunities that other young men around the neighborhood took for granted. Mohammed and Hassan were telling their village leaders that they could now stand on their own two feet.

Johnny heard about Hassan's come-uppance and found it very curious. He had to think back when he was a young man rebelling against his father Charles (**American Revolution**). He remembered how he was so angry that he dumped all of his father's tea into the ocean (**Boston Tea Party**). He thought about the protracted fight with his father that led to him declaring that he was a strong, independent man who was able to take care of himself (**July 4th, 1776—American Independence Day**).

In neighboring Libya, Ali heard about Mohammed and Hassan rebelling against their village chieftains. It seems his village chieftain belonged to the same generation who believed that village chief should rule the village with an iron fist. In fact, Ali's tribal elder Muammar was known as a madman in some circles. Muammar had physically beat Ali many times and was known to go off in verbal tirades. His tirades became known throughout the neighborhood.

Ali challenged the chief to a fight and the chief told him, "Never again will you challenge my authority over this village, you ungrateful bastard!" Then the two of them fought each other to the death. It was heart-wrenching to see chief and indian behaving so brutally toward each other.

In the end, Ali pinned the chief down on the ground and in a grand gesture of compassion, allowed the chief to walk away in defeat. Ali had won and the neighborhood had become a safer place (**Libyan dictator, Muammar Gaddafi, is killed ending his brutal dictatorship**).

The years 2011 and 2012 have witnessed mass Arab uprisings in North Africa, including Tunisia, Egypt, Libya, Bahrain, Syria, and even Iran. The people of these countries demanded the replacement of dictators with more democratic systems of government that reflect the will of the people. Dictators such as Hosni Mubarak in Egypt have ruled by force and intimidation and have not allowed free and open elections. The citizens of these Arab countries have obviously become fed up with living in poverty while the ruling elite live a life of luxury, exploiting the masses.

In late January 2011 in Tunisia, a street vendor named Ali poured gas on himself and burned himself alive. That set the Arab world on fire. Hundreds of thousands of young, unemployed Tunisians began protesting in the streets of Tunis. They were demanding that their ruler, Ben Ali, resign. Ben Ali could not contain the masses and fled the country for the refuge of Saudi Arabia. The winds of freedom were blowing throughout North Africa.

The winds of change then blew across Egypt. There were massive demonstrations of people in the streets of Cairo and Alexandria. These Egyptians were protesting the lack of freedom, poverty, and high rates of unemployment in their country. They marched on Tahrir Square in late January and would not leave until Hosni Mubarak stepped down. The whole country came to a standstill. The stock markets were closed. Public transportation had ground to a halt. Hosni Mubarak's Secret Police did not put up a fight. There were pro-Mubarak protesters who clashed with the demonstrators, but most speculated that Mubarak had assembled his Secret Police to pose as pro-Mubarak demonstrators. On February 11, 2011, Hosni Mubarak officially resigned as dictator of Egypt and millions of Egyptians celebrated in the streets!

The wave of revolution across North Africa then spread to Libya, where the ruthless Colonel Muammar Gaddafi ruled as dictator for over four decades. The people of Libya appeared to have woken up to the fact that Gaddafi had only benefited himself and his family while the people languished in poverty. They had awakened and had taken their collective fate into their own hands.

Libyans had lived in fear of the ruthless dictator and his security forces. Inspired by the brave souls in Tunisia and Egypt, thousands of Libyans banded together to form a strong insurgency against Gaddafi's forces. They placed themselves at great risk of violence and death at the hands of Gaddafi's hired mercenaries who hailed primarily from other countries such as Sudan and Yemen. Gaddafi was known to have sponsored mercenary training camps for years. Libya descended into civil war between forces still loyal to Gaddafi and the rebel insurgency. Many of Libya's ambassadors resigned. Many European countries called for Gaddafi's resignation. German banks froze Libya's funds.

Meanwhile, the United States moved aircraft carriers and warships into the Mediterranean Sea. President Obama stopped short of instituting a no-fly zone because as Secretary of Defense Gates said, "Let's call a spade a spade, if we declare a no-fly zone over Libya, then we are effectively declaring war on Libya." But the North Atlantic Treaty Organization (NATO), led by the United States, did engage in bombing Gaddafi's headquarters in Tripoli.

On October 20, 2011, Muammar Gaddafi was killed near his hometown of Sirte, Libya by the fierce Libyan opposition, sparking wild celebrations that eight months of war finally seemed to be over. Details of the death were hazy but it was announced by several officials of the National Transitional Council (NTC) and backed up by a photograph of a bloodied face ringed by familiar, Gaddafi-style curly hair. Another ruthless Arab dictator had fallen in the Arab Awakening.

The year 2011 turned out to be the year of the mass protest. The freedom won by the people of Tunisia, Egypt and Libya spurred on protests in Bahrain, Syria, and Iran. The new globally interconnected economy instantaneously showcased the freedom and economic opportunity in wealthier societies to those who remained oppressed by dictators. The mechanistic, material age of "might makes right" was giving way to the more balanced age of knowledge and freedom for every individual human being on earth.

The Syrian people recognized they were being exploited by their dictator, Bashar Assad, who was simply following in the footsteps of his father, Hafez Assad. Bashar Assad used his country's military to encircle towns and force his people into submission beginning in early 2011. At least 10,000 Syrians left their homes and crossed the border into Turkey by mid-June, 2011.

However, the Syrian people were ready to continue protesting until their voices are heard and actual changes are made in their government. Since reporters were not allowed into Syria, people outside the country receive reports of the atrocities from amateur video taken by cell phone cameras and uploaded to YouTube and other sites on the Internet. The sheer power of information exchange from individual to individual via the Internet was keeping the Syrian uprising alive.

It seems that the successful grassroots revolutions in Tunisia, Egypt, and Iraq have inspired the masses in other countries such as Syria, Yemen and Bahrain to rise up against dictators who monopolize the wealth and resources of their countries.

The masses in the Middle East spent 2011 and 2012 literally proclaiming to the world that they would no longer tolerate the authoritarian rule of dictators. Individuals made the conscious decision to determine their own fate which resulted in freer societies around the globe. But this process of attaining freedom does not happen overnight and not without hiccups along the road.

There were still two major authoritarian regimes in the world that watched the revolutions in the Middle East very carefully: Saudi Arabia and China. Saudi Arabia began giving away money to its people and also "guaranteed" lifelong employment with the government for all government employees. These actions by the

Saudi regime seem to have quelled any visible unrest in Saudi Arabia, at least for awhile.

Interestingly, Saudi Arabia and China are forging a new relationship at the same time that the United States' relationship with Saudi Arabia has been souring. In essence, Saudi Arabia is divorcing itself from the United States and courting its new suitor, China. This is entirely logical because China has surpassed the United States as the largest consumer of Saudi oil. Both the Saudis and the Chinese benefit handsomely from their newfound fondness for each other. However, both regimes must still contend with the global paradigm shift from the deterministic, top-down Industrial Age to the creative, bottom-up **Age of the Individual**.

MILITARY-INDUSTRIAL-CORPORATE COMPLEX

We in the United States are fortunate to live in a democratic society where every adult has the right to vote. We also have an excellent system of government that was brilliantly designed by our founding fathers. The division of our government into three equal branches of government, the Executive, Legislative and Judicial branches, has served us well and has proven to be a stroke of genius by our Founding Fathers.

However, there are major problems with our system of government. One pervasive problem is the hugely powerful "military-industrial complex," first warned about by President Dwight D. Eisenhower in 1961 in his farewell address to the nation. In that address, President Eisenhower warned the country about the growing power of the monetary relationships between the armed forces, legislators, and the defense industry and their lobbyists.

The United States government is beholden to lobbyists with money representing large corporations and institutions, such as the various factions of the military and the huge defense corporations such as Lockheed International and General Dynamics. According to the Stockholm International Peace research Institute (SIPRI), in 2010 "total world spending on military expenses was $1.531 trillion" and a whopping "46.5 percent of this total, roughly $712 billion, was spent by the United States. (Wikipedia, "Military-industrial complex." http://en.wikipedia.org/wiki/Military-industrial complex, (accessed March 19, 2012))

Similarly, large banks and investment banks such as Goldman Sachs, Morgan Stanley, Citigroup, and Bank of America possess massive influence over the United States government. We are currently living through the battle between the greedy banks and corporations and the individual. Ultimately, the large corporations and institutions of the world will fail without the support of individuals. The military-industrial-corporate complex will ultimately collapse if individuals' rights are not respected.

However, the increasing dominance of the finance industry in the United States' economy cannot easily be overlooked. Since 1960, the financial sector has grown from roughly four percent of GDP to over eight percent. (New York Times online edition, "The Market Mystique," Paul Krugman, http://www.nytimes.com/2009/03/27/opinion/27krugman.html (accessed March 19, 2012))

During the boom years of the 1980's and 1990's, some of the best minds in the United States went into finance. They utilized the concept of "securitization" of loans and mortgages to exponentially expand the profits of financial institutions, all in the name of lowering risk. In actuality, "securitization," which is the dicing, chopping and pureeing of loans and mortgages into new financial instruments, has been exposed as "smoke and mirrors" in the financial collapse of 2008.

The medical-corporate-welfare state will similarly fail if it does not respect the rights of individuals. President Obama was swept into office because he championed the rights of all individuals regardless of race, color, or creed. He was able to pass the healthcare reform bill through the Congress because it championed the rights of each and every American to have affordable healthcare—an entitlement already present in all of the world's industrialized countries except for the United States.

However, Americans will not be able to achieve the lofty goal of affordable healthcare and a basic standard of living for all Americans while at the same time maintaining the role of global policeman. They simply cannot afford it. Americans must make hard choices in the coming years. Only when they shift their priorities toward their own health and well-being will they be able to afford universal healthcare for all Americans.

On June 28, 2012, the United States Supreme Court upheld the constitutionality of President Obama's Affordable Care Act, 5-4, in a landmark decision. (New York Times online edition, "Supreme

Court Upholds Health Care Law, 5-4, in Victory for Obama," Adam Liptak, http://www.nytimes.com/2012/06/29/us/supreme-court-lets-health-law-largely-stand.html (accessed July 1, 2012)) This virtually assured enactment of the law which was passed by both houses of the United States Congress and signed by President Obama.

This ruling was a major victory for President Obama validating the central legislative achievement of his presidency. Chief Justice Roberts wrote in the majority opinion that "The Affordable Care Act's requirement that certain individuals pay a financial penalty for not obtaining health insurance may reasonably be characterized as a tax. Because the Constitution permits such a tax, it is not our role to forbid it, or to pass upon its wisdom or fairness."

As of 2015, "Obamacare" has met with limited success in signing up millions of Americans into private or government health insurance plans. However, millions of Americans have seen their health insurance premiums go up for the same benefits they enjoyed prior to the implementation of "Obamacare."

On a more positive note, President Obama has managed to bring about significant change in healthcare in the United States by mandating over time the use of Electronic Medical Recods (EMR) for physician practices. With over 80% of physician practices and over 90% of hospitals using some form of EMR in 2015, this effort at the digitizing the medical records of patients has met with tremendous success.

As much as the current president, President Trump, has tried to end "Obamacare," there is no turning the clock back. We can only go forward in time and modify and amend the existing healthcare system in the United States.

TRANSATLANTIC TRADE AND INVESTMENT PARTNERSHIP (TTIP)

This proposed legislation aims to consolidate the trade relations between the European Union and the United States into a single transatlantic market by eliminating import tariffs and harmonizing regulation across the Atlantic resulting in the creation of millions of new jobs. The Transnational Institute based in Amsterdam more accurately describes the TTIP as a "political project of a transatlantic corporate and political elite which, on the unfounded promise of increased trade and job creation, will attempt to reverse social and environmental regulatory protections, redirect legal rights from citizens to corporations, and consolidate US and European global leadership in a changing world order.

With over one third of all global trade flowing through the USA and the EU, TTIP would create the world's largest free trading bloc which would have enormous implications for the developing countries of the world which form essentially the other 50% of global GDP. Namely, TTIP would be the preeminent strategy to help regain US and European hegemony vis-à-vis Brazil, Russia, India, China South Africa and the BRICS alliance nations. (Transnational Institute, "Executive Summary," https://www.tni.org/files/download/executive_summary_clear.pdf (accessed September 28, 2015))

According to the Atlantic-Community.org—The Open Think Tank on Foreign Policy—there is a major gap between the interests of consumers and the interests of corporations in this legislation. This organization points to 5 top concerns and criticisms of TTIP:

1) Lack of Transparency
2) Increased Corporate Legal Protection
3) Adverse Economic Impact

4) Decreased Financial Regulation of Corporations
5) Privatization of European Agriculture and Healthcare Industries

The most egregious facet of this legislation is the fact that it is being drafted entirely behind closed doors both in the United States and in the European Union. Any legislation that is purposely hidden from public view necessarily implies that it would be detrimental to the interests of the consumer and should not be trusted.

The second criticism leveled against TTIP is the so-called Investor-State Dispute Settlement mechanism which is likely to be part of the agreement. This mechanism will "enable US companies investing in Europe to challenge EU governments directly at private international tribunals, whenever they find that changes in law in the area of public health, consumer, environmental or social protection interfere with their profits. EU companies investing abroad would have the same privilege in the US," states the Corporate Europe Observatory.

When United States President Eisenhower warned the American people about the dangers of the "military-industrial complex," he was telling Americans to be careful not to allow "big government" and "big business" to collude with one another in the "Fascist Business Model." Well, Americans and Europeans alike are now living in the Fascist Business Model and do not seem to be bothered by it. The TTIP would simply be the crowning achievement of the fascist political and financial elite in hijacking the governments of the United States and Europe. It is everything that President Eisenhower warned against in his famous speech.

Many in Europe also worry that their civil rights and the rights of labor unions would be eroded by this legislation. Some worry that the privatization of portions of the government-run healthcare systems would ensue. Still others wonder if the distinctly American cultural phenomenon of filing lawsuits for anything and everything would be exported to Europe. These issues are not being discussed at all because the entire TTIP legislation is being conducted behind closed doors. Something fishy is surely going on here.

For More Information,
Please Visit www.DollarImplosion.com.

CHAPTER 5

DOLLAR COLLAPSE

*After his devastating divorce, Johnny thought things couldn't get any worse. He was dealing with all of the debt that the courts had placed on him and trying to get his life back in order. Johnny struggled desperately to keep up with all his bills and maxed out credit cards, not to mention trying to stay in shape and keep competing with other younger upstarts such as Minjoon (**South Korea**) and Hiroto (**Japan**). But he just could not manage to keep up with all of the payments. Johnny came to his wit's end. He hoped that he could just keep borrowing from others to pay off his huge mountain of debt.*

Then came the phone calls from the credit card companies when Johnny fell behind on his monthly payments. They called him at all hours. Johnny was able to obtain even more credit cards, which he used to make the minimum payments on the credit cards he had already maxed out. Johnny was robbing Peter to pay Paul. This worked for a couple more years.

*At first, Johnny refused to believe that he was in so much financial trouble (**Skyrocketing U.S. national debt**); he was in denial. Then he got angry at himself for squandering his incredible wealth. How could he have been so stupid? Then he hoped that he could bargain with his creditors, including the bank and the credit card companies. He actually did reduce his debt slightly with this approach.*

But Johnny could read the writing on the wall—he knew that his extravagant lifestyle would not and could not go on forever. He became depressed and began to seriously contemplate bankruptcy. He couldn't bear to think about his financial problems any longer and drifted off into a deep sleep. . .

While Johnny slept, thirteen black government cars pulled up to Johnny's driveway (**Financial Collapse of 2008**). At least twenty men filed out of the cars and massed on Johnny's front porch. The men pounded on the front door and woke Johnny up from his slumber. Johnny knew the day of reckoning had come. His bags were already packed. They had come to repossess all his valuables and his house. He did not put up a fight. He knew the party was over.

Johnny slowly opened the door for the mysterious men and asked who they were. They replied, "We are repo men here to repossess your cars!"(**General Motors and Chrysler declare bankruptcy in 2009**) Johnny pinched himself to see if he was dreaming, but he was not. He let the strangers inside and had a short conversation with them. The men then repossessed all of Johnny's fancy sports cars.

Johnny was left with only his Ford Escape (**Ford Motor Company narrowly escaped bankruptcy**) and was now forced to live less extravagantly. This was a blessing in disguise because the car burned considerably less gas than his fancy sports cars. Johnny couldn't believe this was happening to him and pinched himself to see if this was all a terrible dream. Alas, it was not a dream—he had no choice but to accept his fate. He was not sure if he was going broke or becoming middle-aged or both . . .

THE ALMIGHTY DOLLAR—AMERICA'S BIGGEST EXPORT

The biggest American export to the world is its currency, the dollar. Near the end of World War II, 730 delegates from all 44 Allied nations gathered at the Mount Washington Hotel in Bretton Woods, New Hampshire in the United States, for the United Nations Monetary and Financial Conference. The delegates deliberated upon and signed the Bretton Woods Agreements during the first three weeks of July, 1944. (Wikipedia, "Bretton Woods System," http://en.wikipedia.org/wiki/Bretton_Woods_System (accessed February 16, 2012))

The United States dollar unofficially became the world's reserve currency. In essence, all other countries in the world are paying hidden taxes to the United States by using the dollar—"seigniorage". This is the price that the rest of the world pays for American security.

In a nutshell, this is the winning formula for the United States: expand the reach of American business to the farthest corners of the world and protect those assets with a strong military presence. Or vice versa: invade other countries with or without their permission and then bring in American business interests to reap the booty. Naturally, when U.S. business enters a new geographic area, it brings with it the use of the dollar. This formula has worked well for the American empire.

Ultimately, the glue that holds the whole American empire together is its currency. Conversely, the downfall of the American empire will be the collapse of the dollar. The hegemony of the United States' militaristic empire and the dollar would likely continue if the dollar was sound. But it is not sound and is rapidly declining. Its death blow will come all too quickly.

The dollar is inexorably linked to oil, yielding what some experts call the "petrodollar." The American empire relies heavily on oil for its daily operations. This empire has ingeniously created a global oil market based on the dollar, largely due to the "special" relationship the United States has with the world's largest producer of oil, Saudi Arabia.

This special relationship was initiated by King Abdul Aziz, the founder of modern Saudi Arabia, when he met Franklin D. Roosevelt on the USS Quincy in the Suez Canal on February 14, 1945, and agreed to his country's historic oil-for-security relationship with the United States. (Unger 2004, 3) Simply stated, Saudi Arabia sells its oil on the open market only in U.S. dollars. The United States, in turn, supplies the Saudi government with the weapons it needs to keep its people under control.

Never mind the fact that the Saudi government is one of the most ruthless governments in the world. Also, let's not forget that seventeen of the twenty terrorists in the September 11, 2001 attacks on the United States came from Saudi Arabia.

In fact, many of the relatives of the Saudi royal family and the wealthy Bin Laden family who were in the United States at the time of the attacks were allowed to leave the U.S. on a charter flight sanctioned by the United States government, at a time when all flights were grounded throughout the country. According to Craig Unger, author of *House of Bush House of Saud*, on September 12, 2001, the day after the 9/11 terrorist attacks on the United States,

> *"the Saudi Arabian ambassador to the United States, Prince Bandar bin Sultan bin Abdul Aziz was orchestrating the exodus of more than 140 Saudis scattered throughout the country. They included members of two families: One was the royal House*

of Saud, the family that ruled the kingdom of Saudi Arabia, and which, thanks to the country's vast oil reserves, was without question the richest family in the world. The other family was the Sauds' close friends and allies, the bin Ladens, who in addition to owning a multibillion-dollar construction conglomerate had spawned the notorious terrorist Osama bin Laden..."
(Unger 2004, 2)

However, this special relationship is fraught with contradictions: "The United States, sworn defender of Israel, was also the guarantor of security to the guardians of Wahhabi Islam, the fundamentalist religious sect that was one of Israel's and America's mortal enemies." (Unger 2004, 3) The special relationship between the United States and Saudi Arabia is personified in the relationship between the oil-rich Bush and Saud families.

If the monarchy of Saudi Arabia were to fall, it would have a lasting impact on the United States and the whole world. This is because Saudi Arabia is the world's largest exporter of oil. If the Saudi people were to rise up and demand their share of the oil wealth of their country, there would be dramatic changes in the ownership of the oil resources of Saudi Arabia. In effect, the oil industry in Saudi Arabia would be nationalized. Then the leadership of the country would be free to raise the price of oil as it saw fit. This would surely lead to a permanent increase in the price of oil.

In addition, the new Saudi leadership may not be so beholden to the United States, and may decide to sell their oil for euros or gold. This would be devastating for the American empire, because the empire relies heavily on cheap petrodollars to keep itself afloat. **Petrodollars are the lifeblood of the American empire.** Ultimately, the fall of the Saudi monarchy could be the proverbial straw that breaks the camel's back.

In fact, William R. Clark coined the phrase "petrodollar warfare" referring to the hypothesis that one of the driving forces of United

States foreign policy is maintaining the status of the United States dollar as the world's dominant reserve currency by pricing oil sales in dollars (Clark 2005, 27). According to proponents of this hypothesis,

>   . . .*because most countries rely on oil imports, they are forced to maintain large stockpiles of dollars in order to continue imports. This creates a consistent demand for U.S. dollars and upwards pressure on the dollar's value, regardless of economic conditions in the United States. This in turn allegedly allows the United States government to gain revenues through "seigniorage" and by issuing bonds at lower interest rates than they otherwise would be able to. As a result the United States government can run higher budget deficits at a more sustainable level than can most other countries. A stronger dollar also means that goods imported into the United States are relatively cheap.* (Wikipedia, "Petrodollar warfare," http://en.wikipedia.org/wiki/Petrodollar_warfare (accessed April 20, 2012))

For these reasons, it is crucial to the American empire to protect the current system of pricing oil sales in dollars only and to not allow oil sales in other currencies. **Any country that seeks to sell its oil for anything other than dollars presents a mortal threat to the American Empire**. It seems that most Americans do not understand this important concept. In fact, the entire American media has virtually banned the term "petrodollar" from its reporting since 2007! It seems the Empire does not wish to expose its weak underbelly to anyone including its own citizens.

The most erudite analysis of the dismantling of the petrodollar will not be found anywhere in the mainstream media—it is put forth by Dr. Jim Willie in perhaps his finest article to date, "US Dollar Will Not Survive 2015!" (http://www.silverdoctors.com/jim-willie-us-dollar-will-not-survive-2015/#more-50383, accessed August 27, 2015). In this article, Dr. Willie clearly and succinctly describes the driving forces and key events in the systemic breakdown of the dollar-based financial system. Specifically, Dr. Willie describes the "four legs of the Petro-Dollar as the banking system, the FOREX currencies, the sovereign bonds, and crude oil" and how each leg is failing.

Firstly, the entire **banking system** turned insolvent in 2008. The liquidation of Lehman Brothers was the sacrificial lamb offered by the corrupt banking cabal, but it did not cure the problem of insolvency for the banking industry. They have simply continued as "hollow reed pillars" kept on artificial life support by the federal government's Quantitative Easing (QE) and Zero Interest Rate Policy (ZIRP). The federal government cannot allow any of the big banks to fail because if one big Western bank enters failure, the entire set of big banks will fail simultaneously in direct contagion.

Secondly, all of the **major currencies** are in turmoil now. Emerging market debt is in the trillions because much of it is denominated in US dollars, so when another currency loses value to the dollar, that countries debt skyrockets. They print money to cover their debts and, as a result, their currency loses value. Defaults lie directly ahead for the emerging markets and for the weaker countries in the European Union beginning with Greece.

Thirdly, the **US Treasury and Bond market** is being supported almost entirely by Quantitative Easing, the highly corrosive monetary policy by the US Federal Reserve. Similarly, other major central banks have been doing the same thing including the Bank of England, European Central Bank and the Bank of Japan. At first, the central banks were coordinated in their money printing policies. Lately, they have been acting to preserve their own economies without regard for other countries. Witness the US government raiding the Japanese $1.2 trillion pension fund and the Swiss government deciding to break ranks with the EU by removing the Swiss franc peg to the Euro.

Fourthly, the connection between the US dollar and **Crude Oil** has been broken, largely not described or reported in the press. A vast system of FOREX derivatives are being dissolved that connect to the Crude Oil price. The falling oil price and rising US dollar are evidence that there is a decoupling of the price of oil vis-à-vis the dollar. The relationship between the US government and the Saudis has deteriorated to alarming levels. The "divorce" between the United States and Saudi Arabia is almost complete.

Meanwhile, the Saudis have wasted no time in courting the Chinese in monthly conferences with the Beijing leaders in what could be called a love fest for economic cooperation. The Saudis and other Gulf Emirate nations will be working to convert their combined $2.2 trillion in sovereign wealth funds into diversified non-dollar assets led by Gold. These Arab nations will work to replace their Gold bullion stolen in Swiss banks.

All credit for this analysis goes to Dr. Willie whose courageous work should be commended by all. He is a modern-day oracle for the great masses of humanity and we owe him tremendous gratitude and appreciation for his unwavering pursuit of truth and justice on our planet. Let us be inspired by those who dare speak the truth and take the necessary steps to protect our wealth during this paradigm shift to individual empowerment.

THE SECOND IRAQ WAR

Iraq holds much the same importance as Saudi Arabia. Nearly 20 percent of the world's oil comes from Iraq. Saddam Hussein, the former dictator of Iraq, threatened to sell Iraq's oil for *euros*, not dollars. This would have been disastrous for the American empire, because it would have been the beginning of a slippery slope in which oil was traded in other currencies besides the dollar. Saddam Hussein had made a stab at the weak underbelly of the American empire, but the empire struck back with a vengeance.

Had Saddam Hussein been allowed to sell his country's oil for euros, America would have lost its monopoly on petrodollars, which would have had major consequences for the American empire. This is why President George Bush, Sr. and President George W. Bush fought desperately to overthrow Saddam Hussein, a man the U.S. administration once supported. On a personal level, their familial ties to the House of Saud would have lessened in importance, as well.

Thus, the U.S. administration under President George W. Bush fabricated the story that Iraq possessed "weapons of mass destruction," and the United States invaded a sovereign country, resulting in the loss of over one hundred thousand Iraqi lives and over five thousand American and coalition lives. Not to mention the hundreds of billions of dollars in cost to the American empire. However, this war was totally in keeping with the idea of a continuously expanding empire. That is, empires must continually expand or face rapid decline.

Many readers will recall the widespread abuse of military prisoners in the Abu Ghraib prison during the Second Iraq War. In late 2003, Amnesty International and the Associated Press published reports of a series of human rights violations against detainees in the Abu Ghraib prison in Iraq perpetrated by the United States Army and the Central Intelligence Agency. According to Wikipedia, "these violations included physical and sexual abuse, torture, rape sodomy and murder. The incidents received widespread condemnation both within the United States and around the world, although some conservative media outlets supported these barbaric methods of the United States war machine.

President George W. Bush did his best to portray these incidents as isolated events, but human rights organizations such as the Red Cross, Amnesty International and Human Rights Watch declared that "the abuses at Abu Ghraib were not isolated but were part of a wider pattern of torture and brutal treatment at American overseas detention centers, including those in Iraq, Afghanistan, and Guantanamo Bay. There was evidence that authorization for the torture had come from high up in the military hierarchy, with allegations that Secretary of Defense Donald Rumsfeld had authorized some of the techniques. (Wikipedia, "Abu Ghraib torture and prisoner abuse," https://en.wikipedia.org/wiki/Abu_Ghraib_torture_and_prisoner_abuse, (accessed September 27, 2015))

The United States had become the fascist oppressor that it had opposed so successfully in World War II. Many honest, law-abiding citizens of the United States were ashamed of the atrocities committed by their government and the tide turned against the war quickly. Barack Obama made "ending the war in Iraq" a major plank of his successful bid for the Presidency of the United States in 2008. The American public had been duped by their own government and collectively decided that it had had enough of the war and the lies and torture that accompanied it.

Iran is crucially important for the exact same reasons as Iraq. That is, if Iran is allowed to sell or somehow succeeds in selling its oil for euros, it will be destabilizing for the American empire, whose foundation is the petrodollar. However, the cracks in the dam began appearing in 2011 when Iran went so far as forming a rival market for the trade of oil in euros, based in the Persian Gulf with the backing of Russia and China.

The Iranian Oil Bourse is scheduled to open for daily operations in September 2012—the exact time frame that the United States or its proxy, Israel, have threatened to attack Iran under the pretense of Iran building nuclear weapons. This argument sounds eerily similar to the lie which President George W. Bush fed to the American people prior to invading Iraq in 2003. (Wikipedia, "Petrodollar warfare," http://en.wikipedia.org/wiki/Petrodollar_warfare (accessed March 28, 2012))

Thus, the real threat of Iran to the United States is that it may decide not to play the petrodollar game of the United States. This would be a mortal threat to the American empire because it would set the precedent for other oil-rich countries to sell their oil in currencies other than the dollar. The idea that Iran will be a nuclear threat to the West, even with its development of nuclear power capabilities, is merely a façade for the real threat to the weak underbelly of the American empire, the ***petrodollar***.

Eventually, the petrodollar monopoly will fail. Either the impending dollar implosion will spur the sale of oil in euros or gold, or vice versa. These momentous events in history will be like a one-two punch to the wavering United States. The final knockout punch will come just a few short years later, when the U.S. government either defaults or rewrites the rules of the financial game. Then the government will have no choice but to form a global, electronic currency based on gold, by merging the U.S. dollar, the euro, and the yen or yuan.

Still, the two largest bubbles, the dollar bubble and the government debt bubble, have yet to pop. When the dollar bubble bursts beginning in late 2019 and continuing through 2023, we will witness an historic event that will never be repeated. It will be the fall of the twin towers of the global economy and all of the world's central banks will not be able to find a solution.

There will be massive loss of confidence in the dollar in the United States which will result in a "run" on the dollar. This will happen unexpectedly and very quickly, probably lasting only a few days. The massive outflow of capital from the United States will lead to further collapse of the stock market and the real estate market. The government will again drastically increase the money supply, which will lead to higher inflation and interest rates, which will lead to further loss of confidence in the dollar, and so on in a downward death spiral.

When America's foreign creditors, including China, Japan, Korea, and others see this happening, they will scramble to sell their remaining dollars (US Treasuries and Bonds) for gold or other currencies, which will further erode the value of the dollar, contributing further to the downward spiral of the dollar. The silver lining is that U.S. dollar debt will be significantly reduced with the collapse of the dollar. That is, if the dollar loses 30 percent of its value relative to gold or other currencies, then suddenly the value of the dollars that foreigners and Americans hold is worth 30 percent less, and the value of the U.S. national debt is 30 percent less than it was before the "***dollar implosion***."

The reason the dollar will ultimately collapse is that the underlying U.S. and global economic system is out of balance, and the only way to rebalance the entire system will be to evolve to a global currency.

There are many arguments advanced against the eventual collapse of the dollar:

- The United States is too big to fail—that is, other countries around the world rely so heavily on the United States market that it is in their best interest to not let the dollar bubble pop. But the reality is that no one country controls the market, not even China. So it is in each individual nation's own interest to get out of the dollar, i.e. "last one out is a rotten egg."
- There is no other currency that could take the place of the dollar as the world's reserve currency—that is, no other currency in existence today. However, a new digital, global currency managed by a world central bank will lead to increased stability in global economic trade in the long run.

In fact, as of the end of 2010, the dollar had already lost roughly 30 percent of its value relative to the euro within a decade. Interestingly, the Euro Zone was dealing with the potential debt default and bankruptcy of its weakest states contemporaneously with the declining value of the dollar. The fact that Europe was struggling with its own sovereign debt issues at the same time as the United States actually strengthens the argument that the rich Western industrialized countries are all "going broke."

The underlying fundamental economic changes in the United States will continue to play themselves out until the debt problem has been solved. As the U.S. economic bubbles burst and the world's economy slows, investors will invest their money where the returns are greater. As a matter of fact, the largest purchaser of U.S. Treasuries at the quarterly auctions is now the Federal Reserve. In fact, the Federal Reserve's balance sheet is nearly $5 trillion.

However, the Federal Reserve has begun a rebalancing of its balance sheet starting in 2015. It is actually engaging in Quantitative Tightening, the opposite of Quantitative Easing, by actually removing roughly $60 billion per month from the money supply. Both Quantitative Easing and Quantitative Tightening have never been tried on such a grand scale, but the results are encouraging thus far. . .

The pain will only get worse from here. The final bubble to burst will be the mother of them all, the government debt bubble. This will likely happen several years after the dollar bubble has popped. When the dollar bubble bursts, there will be a sharp decline in available capital due to massive capital outflows from the United States and due to the further negative effects on the real estate, stock market, and private equity bubbles. The Federal Reserve will try to keep the economy from freezing up by printing even larger amounts of dollars, but this will lead to higher inflation.

However, unlike the situation with AIG or Bear Stearns, the United States government will be the one in trouble. This will lead to failed Treasury auctions because outside investors will have lost confidence in the U.S. economy. Then the government will be faced either with defaulting on its debt payments or cranking up the printing presses resulting in hyperinflation.

Most likely, the United States government will do both: it will drastically increase the money supply by printing massive amounts of dollars, and then will be forced to default on its massive debt. When the government defaults later this decade, it will have to drastically cut expenses across the board and raise taxes. No government program will be spared.

Many experts believe that major "non-discretionary" items in the budget, including Defense, Medicare/Medicaid, and Social Security, will all be cut by at least 50 percent or more. Discretionary spending will be cut even further. In addition, the personal income tax rate would also have to increase to 40 to 50 percent for all Americans. (Wiedemer et al 2010, 210-13)

The bursting of the dollar bubble will change our lives forever. We will finally be forced to live according to our means as a nation, after the fallout has cleared. Much of our wealth will have evaporated and we will not be able to re-inflate the bubbles by simply printing more money. We will learn firsthand what it feels like for a nation to go bankrupt. Even so, it will not be the end of the world, but merely a new beginning.

How will this affect our daily lives? All dollar-based securities and assets such as stocks, bonds, annuities, and life insurance plans will lose tremendous value. Those living on fixed incomes will have a particularly difficult time making ends meet. Only those people who have converted their dollar-based assets to gold or silver will do well. Residential and commercial real estate values will also take a hit because they are dollar-based, as well.

The single most important thing Americans can do is to shift their assets away from dollar-based assets such as stocks, bonds, and U.S. Treasuries into gold, silver, and commodities. The smart money is going into gold and silver in droves. When enough people around the world shift their wealth into gold and silver, the dollar will implode. By then, it will be too late to take action, as trillions of dollars of wealth will have vanished into thin air.

This situation is not for the faint of heart. But if you take action before the dollar implosion, you will end up on sound footing. Millions of Americans lost trillions of dollars in the real estate crash and financial meltdown of 2008. Hopefully, if you take the necessary steps of eliminating debt and converting your stocks and bonds into gold, silver and commodity-based assets, you will protect your life savings. You must act before the dollar implodes!

For More Information,
Please Visit www.DollarImplosion.com.

CHAPTER 6

WORLDWIDE BANKING SYSTEM COLLAPSE

Meanwhile, Johnny's compatriots Karl, Oliver and Nicholas were getting fat and lazy, as well. Karl was still in good shape for a fifty year-old man. But he did not have the same energy of his youth. Oliver was a couple years younger than Karl, but was in no better shape. Nicholas married a former porn star who was half his age! All of these men had seen better days.

*Both Karl and Nicholas had loaned a lot of money to their dear friend Giorgos (**Greece**), but Giorgos was not prudent with the money. He ended up losing all of the money his friends had lent him and he went even deeper into debt. Giorgos simply could not pay Karl and Nicholas back, so his friends agreed to forgive most of the debt (**Greek bail-out of 2012**). Karl and Nicholas lost a lot of money in the process. This was the last thing they needed, especially since they were going through middle age troubles themselves.*

The fact of the matter was that Johnny and his best friends in the neighborhood had become wealthy through hard work during their 20s, 30s and 40s. Middle age crept up on all of them and they soon became relatively less productive than in decades past. However, each of them still continued to live a life of luxury by charging their expenses on credit cards. It seemed there was no limit to how much they could borrow.

But just as Johnny was going through near-bankruptcy and dealing with the accompanying grieving process, his friends who were all of his generation were dealing with similar issues. Johnny became depressed. Karl, Oliver and Nicholas looked at their own predicament and they became depressed, too (**Europe and the United States enter a protracted period of economic malaise beginning in 2008**). It seemed the economic malaise of these middle-aged men was contagious and spreading to the whole neighborhood. They wondered if the entire dollar-based system of exchange would break down, since Johnny was the one who set it up in the first place.

Then all hell broke loose. A young upstart named Afshin (**Iran**) challenged Johnny's supremacy, not with brute force, but by defying Johnny's edict that all petroleum will be bought and sold in dollars. Afshin expressly stated that he would sell his oil for bartered services and currencies other than the dollar. Johnny knew that if Afshin was successful, he would be dealt a mortal blow which would lead to the end of his empire. Johnny rattled his saber and threatened to attack Afshin if he went through with his plan But Afshin was dead serious and did not back down.

Afshin created the International Oil Bourse which began the public exchange of oil for any currency in the neighborhood. Johnny had no choice but to attack Afshin. They exchanged blows like two heavyweight boxers in a championship fight. Johnny was wiser and more experienced, but did not possess the stamina of the younger, more powerful Afshin. They fought valiantly, but neither one could knock the other out. It was a draw. However, the damage was done. The entire neighborhood broke into chaotic anarchy. Nobody was sure who made the rules in this brave new world.

Then, Chen (**China**), Carlos (**Brazil**), Ashish (**India**) had the brilliant idea of developing a new currency and using it for trade among themselves and with Afshin. In fact, that's exactly what they did. At first, Karl, Oliver, and Nicholas laughed at their idea. But their idea caught on like wildfire. Many others including Nguyen and Hiroto began to trade in the new currency.

*Soon there was economic chaos in the neighborhood! There were two different currencies in the neighborhood and other currencies were being developed by Minjoon (**South Korea**) and Mehmet (**Turkey**). The dollar-based system of exchange had broken down and nobody trusted anybody (**The Coming Worldwide Banking Collapse**) . . .*

FIAT CURRENCY PROBLEM

Since the dollar is a fiat currency manipulated by the Federal Reserve, it is doomed to failure. Fiat currency simply means that the only thing backing it is the government's word; that is, the currency is government controlled. History is littered with worthless fiat currencies, including that of the infamous Weimar Republic of Germany during World War I. The French franc went through hyperinflation twice in the 1700s. The currencies of Argentina and Turkey went through hyperinflation in the 1990s.

Americans have witnessed the fate of other fiat currencies, but have assumed that this could never happen to them. But the stage is being set for this monumental historical event which many experts believe may begin in the latter of this decade (2016 to 2020). The cold, hard reality is that we in the United States are headed for higher rates of inflation, higher unemployment, and at least some social unrest. The rest of the world will suffer greatly, as well.

Americans have been witnessing the slow and steady demise of the "Almighty Dollar" since President Nixon took the United States off the gold standard in 1971. The question simply remains, when and how will the dollar be dealt its death blow. It has become clear that the demise of the dollar is driven by the increasing debt of the United States government, which grows continuously with annual trillion dollar deficits. In March 2012, the U.S. national debt surpassed $15 trillion, which is about 100 percent of the United States GDP.

History teaches us that all empires collapse because they ultimately generate unsustainable debt. The booming far eastern nations of China and Japan, and have become the bankers to the United States. They hold the largest amounts of U.S. Treasuries. It will simply take less demand for the dollar, i.e. U.S. Treasuries, for the dollar to fail. When it finally fails, it will seem like it happened quickly, but in reality, the dollar has been increasingly losing value for over four decades.

Growing up in the booming automotive Mecca of Detroit, Michigan in the 1970s and 80s, I never thought that our currency, the mighty U.S. dollar, might one day become extinct. I still have difficulty accepting this possibility. But the fact of the matter is that all fiat currencies eventually fail due to government mismanagement. *The dollar is no exception.*

This process is simply pure economics at work. Just as we individually have maximum credit limits beyond which we default on our loans or file for bankruptcy, governments have credit limits beyond which they default or claim insolvency. According to the authors of *Aftershock*, our national credit limit is between $15 and $25 trillion. We are currently, in 2015, adding roughly $1 trillion annually to our national debt, so we have roughly five to seven years before our credit dries up. Then we will be faced with the prospect of hyperinflation or government default.

Historically, empires have never willingly abandoned their currency, so we will eventually endure high rates of unemployment and inflation and high interest rates before the collapse of the dollar and the subsequent collapse of the U.S. government debt bubble.

I believe that we are living in a bubble economy, as was brilliantly elucidated by David Wiedemer, PhD, in *America's Bubble Economy* (2006) and *Aftershock* (2010). Our bubble economy relies on printing money without gold backing. So we have witnessed the rapid growth of the real estate, stock market, and private equity bubbles and the inevitable bursting of these bubbles in late 2008. Dr. Wiedemer called this the "Bubblequake."

PLAYING FIELD IS LEVELED

After the collapse and devaluation of the U.S. dollar in this decade, the mother of all bubbles, the government debt bubble, will finally burst leading to the collapse of the entire global banking system. This means that the world's bankers will have to devise a world central bank and will have to create a new world currency. The playing field will be leveled and all of the world's countries will have to play by the same rules.

This will affect Americans the most, because we will be forced to live according to our means, rather than simply printing more money. Banks and other businesses will fail. People in the United States and throughout the world will suffer due to ever-increasing rates of inflation, reflected in the increasing price of goods and services. The pain of worsening inflation will not subside until the new world banking system along with a new set of rules and new global currency has been established.

Immediately after the United States government defaults on its debt obligations, central bankers around the world will gather together and formally create a new digital global currency based on gold. Each citizen, business, and institution will have to trade their local currency for the new gold-based currency, based on agreed upon exchange rates at that time. Those holding American dollars will lose a huge percentage of the nominal value of the currency. Other currencies like the Chinese yuan and the Indian rupee will instantaneously gain value when traded in for the hypothetical digital gold-based currency.

In reality, this process of the collapse of banking institutions and central banks throughout the world will lead to a more integrated system that will prevent banking system collapse in the future. This is a process of evolution to a global currency and globally integrated system of finance. No one player will make the rules for the rest of the world. The system will transform itself into a more equitable system whereby each player plays by the same rules. The banking industry will finally have been brought to its knees.

The wars in Syria and Ukraine are last ditch efforts by the banker cabal to delay the "global currency reset" which is a euphemism for the collapse of the dollar as the world's reserve currency and the return of the Gold Standard. However, the evolution of our species is not dictated by a select few wealthy families, but by the continual growth, evolution and contributions of each and every individual to the collective consciousness.

The return of the Gold Standard is the rebalancing of our entire system of wealth and power which is undergoing a dramatic shift to the developing world on a macro level and to the individual on a micro level. The developing world will soon complete their creation of a more fair and equitable global economic system based on the Gold Standard rather than the old system whose rules were dictated by elite bankers in New York and London. The individual, too, will have a much better chance at freeing himself or herself from the chains of debt slavery with the imminent return of the Gold Standard.

The large banks around the world are like ruthless dictators. They impose their will on their patrons and keep the lion's share of profit to themselves. But the coming dollar implosion will force the entire banking industry to realign itself with the welfare of its patrons. Gold will be the ultimate store of value for many years after the dollar implosion, which will mean drastically reduced profits for the banking industry as a whole.

Many banking institutions will be forced to close their doors. Only the banks that are the most egalitarian will survive. This will be the ultimate revenge for those who have been inhumanely treated by the banks. It will be a huge victory for the common man, the global citizen who plays by the rules. The huge payouts to Wall Street will be gone forever.

The financial industry has become corrupt to the point of ruining the world economy. In 2011, the United States government finally began prosecuting major banks such as Chase Morgan and Goldman Sachs for selling risky mortgage-backed securities to credit unions when they knew they were essentially worthless. However, the federal government is so thoroughly infiltrated with Wall Street cronies that this entire exercise amounted to a slap on the wrist.

Ann Barnhardt, formerly of Barnhardt Management, became so disenchanted with the utter corruption on Wall Street that, in 2011, she closed the doors of the independent brokerage company she had started eight years ago. In an interview with Jim Puplava in 2011, Barnhardt blasts the entire Wall Street establishment for its greed and moral turpitude:

"The only lesson that these criminal degenerates learned from the 2008 situation was that they could do anything they want and that pimp daddy government would bail them out. . . You have to get your heads around the fact that there are truly evil people in the world who do not give a crap about anyone or anything except themselves, their own personal wealth and their own personal power. And they would sell their grandmother to the Nazis for a nickel without hesitation if they thought they could get away with it. . . And we now know that the government is absolutely stuffed to the gills almost exclusively with this same type of moral degenerate culture. These people that are in the government—not just the Congress and Executive Branch but also in the bureaucracy—they are in it for themselves. They are in it for the money. . .

They will do anything. They will steal. They will lie. They will cheat. They will lie to your face. They will look in the camera with this tremendous earnestness and lie with fork tongues through their teeth in order to advance their wealth and power. And if we, as a people, don't get real about this, if we keep having these Pollyanna visions that these people are all on our side and they are really looking out for us. And they are doing the best they can. We will be cork screwed into the ground and this nation will be reduced to a smoldering rubble. You've got to wake up." (Financial Sense, "Transcript for Ann Barnhardt Interview," http://www.financialsense.com/contributors/2011/12/02/ann-barnhardt/interview-transcript (accessed September 21, 2015))

The tables are now turned. This is the Information Age, the age of individual empowerment. The banks and Wall Street will have been given a "forbearance agreement," and if they fail to live up to the terms of the agreement, the public will demand payment in full. President Obama has tried to force the banks to play fair, but with only limited success. In early 2012, the president barely managed to name a leader to the new Consumer Protection Agency for fear that the Republicans in Congress would not confirm his nominee.

The banks will not be able to live up to the reforms placed on them by the United States government and the American people will demand that they pay their debt to the consumer in full. They will walk away from their mortgages in droves. Then the American public will take action by shifting its wealth out of dollars and into gold en masse. In America, there's a saying, "The customer is always right." The banks have failed to satisfy their customers and they will pay dearly. The banks need the customer more than the customer needs the banks.

The Europeans have been living through their own financial meltdown. On November 27, 2010, thousands of protesters marched on the streets of Dublin protesting their government's four-year austerity plan. The Irish government had negotiated a $113 billion loan from the EU and IMF to save the country from bankruptcy, in return for a four-year austerity plan that included tax hikes and budget cuts. One Irish protester said, "We are protesting against the huge debts that are being imposed on us now...I do not know when we are ever going to come out of this." (Voice of America News, "Thousands of Irish Protest Austerity Measures," November 27, 2010)

Greece is all but bankrupt and needs hundreds of billions of euros just to stay afloat. The wealthy members of the European Union, Germany and France, have emphatically stated that they will loan Greece the money, but Greece will have to raise taxes and undertake severe austerity measures, including budget cuts, less vacation, and raising the retirement age to sixty-two. The people often protested in the streets of Athens over the harshness of these austerity measures. They have blamed the politicians and the bankers alike for their predicament. Ultimately, they have nobody to blame but themselves.

Similarly, Spain endured massive demonstrations by young people as the so-called "May 15 Movement" took to the streets in June 2011. The protests focused on Spain's 21 percent unemployment rate, the highest in the industrialized world at the time, and also on the government's economic austerity measures. The movement took its name from the opening round of protests on May 15, 2011.

Eva Fernandez, a social worker marching down Madrid's main boulevard, la Castellana, said, "This capitalistic system doesn't work. It's an unfair system and a lot of people are in a very bad situation, without money." (Goodman 2011) This same sentiment was echoed by the Occupy Wall Street movement a few months later in September 2011. The deeper worry in the European Union is that if one of its members defaults on its debt, the defaults could spread to other economically troubled members (Portugal, Ireland, Italy, Greece, and Spain), resulting in the collapse of the euro and the European Union. This is not a matter to be taken lightly, as it would have global ramifications, similar to what would happen when the U.S. dollar collapses.

Therefore, the term "default" was never used by the European Union when the Greeks were bailed out in early 2012 and again in late 2015. It seems the global banking cartel will do everything in its power to keep the present economic system intact. Ultimately, the United States and the European Union are in the same boat and they will eventually arrive at forming a shared international global electronic currency to their mutual benefit.

For More Information,
Please Visit www.DollarImplosion.com.

ACT III

BIRTH OF THE NEW WORLD ORDER

CHAPTER 7

NEW ECONOMIC PLATFORM

*Uncle Sam, Johnny's beloved uncle, had a different plan for Johnny. He figured that Johnny could stay "King of the World" if he could somehow flood the market with dollars. Johnny took Uncle Sam's advice and began to print dollars like there was no tomorrow (**United States government begins Quantitative Easing in 2012**). But these dollars were not for the benefit of the neighborhood. No, these dollars were exclusively for Johnny and his family and the elite banking cabal. The average man in Johnny's neighborhood (**United States of America**) was working harder for less pay—if he even had a job at all!*

*Oliver (**England**), Nicholas (**France**), and Hiroto (**Japan**) all began to follow Johnny's lead and print gobs and gobs of their own currency. All fiat currencies were in a race to the bottom. Even Chen (**China**) got in on the act, although Chen could afford to do so because he had built up enormous reserves. Karl (**Germany**) was the sole holdout among Johnny's buddies. Karl had been down that road before (**WWII**) and could not bring himself to ruin his livelihood for Johnny's sake.*

*Meanwhile, Chen was creating a network of new relationships with almost everybody in the neighborhood. Chen was meeting with almost every kid in the neighborhood and setting up new deals (**bilateral currency "swap facilities"**) that did not require use of Johnny's "almighty" dollar. Johnny watched in amazement as Chen went about* *forging relationships with nearly everybody in the neighborhood, but there was nothing he could do about it. Chen had built up tremendous wealth and Johnny was in debt up to his eyeballs! It was as if Chen was a diligent spider methodically constructing a web.*

*Chen then decided to take it a step further by creating parallel institutions to the ones Johnny had created. So he created a new bank called the **Asian Infrastructure Investment Bank** to rival the World Bank and Oliver (**England**), Karl (**Germany**), Nicholas (**France**), Giovanni (**Italy**), Ronan (**Australia**) and even Hiroto (**Japan**) signed on to become founding members of this new bank.*

*Chen and his closest buddies--Paulo (**Brazil**), Alexander (**Russia**), Ashish (**India**), and Oscar (**South Africa**)—decided to create the **Asian Development Fund** to rival Johnny's International Monetary Fund. Chen developed the **Shanghai Gold Exchange** to rival Johnny's New York Gold Exchange. He created his own credit card, **UNIONPAY**, that grew to be larger than VISA and MASTERCARD! Alexander and Chen even formed a new system of bank transfers, **CIPS**, to rival Johnny's SWIFT system.*

*It seemed as if the whole neighborhood (**world**) was in cahoots against Johnny. And in a way, they were. The other kids in the neighborhood were simply sick and tired of being bullied by Johnny, so they finally decided that together they could form their own system that was more fair and equitable for all, not just a select few (**Johnny and Oliver**). Johnny's entire infrastructure was breaking down and there was nothing he could do about it. Chen and the rest of the neighborhood were like a giant tsunami that was unstoppable. . .*

THE GOLDEN JACKASS: DR. JIM WILLIE

One of the oracles of the coming collapse of the US dollar and the return of the gold standard is Jim Willie, Ph.D. who publishes his analysis in his monthly newsletter, The Hat Trick Letter, on his website—www.goldenjackass.com. Dr. Willie's keen insight into the current plight of the dollar and the entire central bank fiat currency system is unparalleled.

In an erudite article published on April 25, 2014 entitled *Guide: Pathogenesis and Change Factors*, Dr. Willie lays out his theory of how the elite "banker cabal" has been behind numerous key turning point events in recent US history. In the concluding paragraph of that article, Dr. Willie sums up the solution to the problem of fascist control of the entire power structure of the United States by the "banker cabal" as follows:

*"The solution is not to be found at the doorstep of central banks, since they are the perpetrators of the systemic ruin. They escape prosecution since they appoint the prosecutors. The solution is a return to the Gold Standard, the introduction of new gold-backed currencies, the installation of new banking systems instead of SWIFT, and the construction of free trade zones. They will all be put in place, led by the Eastern superpowers. They will arrive with a vast new structure of legitimacy. They will include barter systems and decentralized mechanisms. They will include new Letters of Credit based in Gold Trade Notes. But the East led by the BRICS nations and their armada of associate nations will be the promoters, installers, and participants of the new strong viable Gold Standard system that the United States dreads and fears. **The West led by Wall Street and London will continue its rapacious confiscation of wealth and its vicious devotion to war until the platform they stand on collapses, built upon US Dollar, US Treasury Bond, and SWIFT copyrights.**"*

Dr. Willie emphatically states that the whole world outside of the United States is rejecting the dollar because it has become worthless.

The Federal Reserve Bank has become the buyer of last resort of US Treasuries and Bonds because the rest of the world no longer wishes to buy them. The Federal Reserve has nearly $5 trillion of debt on its books and is insolvent for all practical purposes. Interestingly, the rest of the world is fully aware of the predicament of the United States dollar as global reserve currency.

He often refers to the coming Dethroning of King Dollar by Emperor Yuan. In fact, he goes on to assert that there will be a "Global Reset" in which the United States will be forced to create a new dollar printed by the United States Treasury which will be devalued by 30% followed by a subsequent 30% devaluation resulting in a 50% loss of value of the dollar. This translates into a doubling of the gold price and a tripling of the price of silver relative to the dollar!

In this excerpt from a recent article published on SilverDoctors. Com, Dr. Willie details the manner in which the Gold Standard will be re-born and also predicts that the United States will have no choice but to create a new Treasury Dollar for domestic use which he has termed the "Scheiss Dollar," (English translation "Shit Dollar"):

"The Gold Standard will arrive from the trade ramps, not the FOREX window. Then later, global banking systems will discard the US Treasuries held in reserve. The event will trigger QE4, and collapse the Western central bank franchise system. Then comes the new Scheiss Dollar on a contrived platter. Gold will win, just a question of when, how, and the depth of global economic destruction."

Dr. Willie bases his predictions on careful analysis of factual events. He has written extensively about China's bilateral currency swap facilities with over 25 countries. China first approached Brazil in 2006 with the plan to settle trade accounts in Chinese Yuan and Brazilian Real—deliberately avoiding the use of the US Dollar for their commerce. It was a simple system: 3 or 4 big Chinese banks had an agreement with 3 or 4 large Brazilian banks to settle their monthly trade accounts in their respective currencies.

However, the bilateral swap facilities between China and numerous other countries was just the beginning. The Chinese were building a whole new economic system to rival the current international dollar-based system and they were doing it in typical Chinese fashion--*they were reverse engineering the Western financial system with their own analogous entities*:

1) New Development Bank (BRICS Bank) to rival the World Bank
2) Asian Infrastructure Investment Bank to rival the International Monetary Fund
3) BRICS Contingent Reserve Arrangement
4) Shanghai Gold Exchange to rival the London Gold Exchange
5) Chinese Debt Ratings Agencies such as Dagong to rival Standard & Poors, Moody's and Fitch rating agencies
6) Chinese Credit Card UnionPay to rival Visa and Mastercard
7) Chinese International Payment System (CIPS) to rival the SWIFT international money transfer system

NEW DEVELOPMENT BANK ("BRICS BANK")

Let's start with the New Development Bank which is located in Shanghai, China. Wikipedia defines the NDB as follows: "The New Development Bank, formerly referred to as the BRICS Development Bank, is a multilateral development bank operated by the BRICS states (Brazil, Russia, India, China and South Africa) as an alternative to the existing US-dominated World Bank and International Monetary Fund. The bank is set up to foster greater financial and development cooperation among the five emerging markets."

"Together, the four original BRIC countries comprise in 2014 more than 3 billion people or 41.4 percent of the world's population, cover more than a quarter of the world's land area over three continents, and account for more than 25 percent of global GDP. The bank will be headquartered in Shanghai, China. Unlike the World Bank, which assigns votes based on capital share, in the New Development Bank each participant country will be assigned one vote and none of the countries will have veto power." (Wikipedia, "New Development Bank," http://en.wikipedia.org/wiki/New_Development_Bank (accessed April 29, 2015))

Just as the United States hosts the World Bank in Washington, DC, China has created a counterweight in the BRICS Bank which it hosts in Shanghai, the financial equivalent of New York. We are witnessing the arrival of the world's newest financial hub, Shanghai, which will rival London, Frankfurt, New York and Tokyo. Soon, Shanghai will be the world's top destination for finance and trade. Americans will want to visit Shanghai simply to get a glimpse of the future of global trade and finance.

Next, we have the Asian Infrastructure Investment Bank which was launched in Beijing in October 2014. Much to the chagrin of the United States, all major countries in the world have signed on to become founding members of this new bank, except for the United States and Japan.

Wikipedia defines this new institution as follows: "The Asian Infrastructure Investment Bank (AIIB) is an international financial institution proposed by the government of China. The purpose of the multilateral development bank is to provide finance to infrastructure projects in the Asian region. Some analysts regard the AIIB as a rival to the IMF, the World Bank and the Asian Development Bank, which are regarded as dominated by developed countries like the United States."

Regardless of the view of the United States which sees these fledgling institutions as threats to its hegemony, the United Nations has addressed the launch of the AIIB as "scaling up financing for sustainable development" for the concern of Global Economic Governance. Chinese Premier Li Keqiang affirms AIIB's cooperative stance. As of April 15, 2015, almost all Asian countries and most major countries outside Asia had joined the AIIB, except the United States, Japan and Canada.

On June 29, 2015, representatives of 50 countries gathered in Beijing to sign the legal framework agreement to establish the $100 billion AIIB. China will have 30.4 percent share of the AIIB's equity, followed by India at 8.5% and Russia at 6.7 %. Key NATO allies of the United States like Germany, France and England decided to join the AIIB, too. Germany will have the largest non-Asian share with 4.1%.

The AIIB will symbolize the rise of China as a global financial powerhouse providing the financing for the world's largest infrastructure projects in the coming years. The Western nations that have opted in to the AIIB simply do not want to miss out on getting a share of the funds that will be disbursed by the AIIB. The two major holdouts who have not joined the AIIB are the United States and Japan. Why? Because the World Bank and the Asian Development Bank which are dominated by the United States and Japan, respectively, would see their effectiveness undercut by this new institution. In other words, both the United States and Japan have the most to lose as this new Chinese-led global development bank takes root.

CONTINGENT RESERVE ARRANGEMENT

The New Development Bank or BRICS Bank, led by China, has created a special fund called the Contingent Reserve Arrangement (CRA) to help prevent balance of payments crises in the coming years. Let's examine CRA a bit more in depth. At the 7th BRICS summit in July 2014, the BRICS countries of Brazil, Russia, India, China and South Africa established the Treaty for the Establishment of a BRICS Contingent Reserve Arrangement in Fortaleza, Brazil.

The objective of this reserve is to provide protection against global liquidity pressures. This includes currency issues where members' national currencies are being adversely affected by global financial pressures. The capital of $100 billion is distributed among the five BRICS countries in Chart 3. (Wikipedia, "BRICS Contingent Reserve Arrangement," https://en.wikipedia.org/wiki/BRICS_Contingent_Reserve_Arrangement, (accessed August 17, 2015))

Country	Capital contribution[5] (billion USD)	Access to Funds (billion USD)	Voting Rights (%)[6]
Brazil	18	18	18.10
China	41	21	39.95
India	18	18	18.10
Russia	18	18	18.10
South Africa	5	10	5.75
Grand Total	100	85	100.00

Chart 3: The distribution, access to funds and voting rights of the Contingent Reserve Arrangement (CRA).

The entire purpose of the CRA is to prevent the currencies of the BRICS & Alliance nations from collapsing as they did in 1997. The BRICS nations and the developing world are now enduring massive downward pressures on their currencies caused by the paradoxical rise in the value of the US dollar.

Why is the dollar paradoxically rising in value if it is nearing collapse? It is rising in value because the entire planet's fiat currency system is failing. In other words, all fiat currencies are rapidly being devalued. The last man standing is the US dollar, but it too will suffer the fate of the rest of the world's fiat currencies. This is why the dollar will rise and rise and rise some more, until it completely dies. Dr. Willie uses the analogy of a dead man floating at sea—his body swells and swells until it eventually bursts!

The World Gold Council (WGC) estimates that demand for gold bullion in China will likely reach 1,000 tons this year. But the price of gold is fixed in New York and London. As a result, Beijing has given the green light to the Shanghai Gold Exchange (SGE) to establish gold-fixing to be denominated in Chinese renminbi (RMB) currency by the end of 2015, while offshore investors can open gold accounts in the Shanghai Free Trade Zone in September 2015.

The Chairman of the Shanghai Gold Exchange, Xu Luode, emphatically states, "We need gold-fixing in RMB. We have a U.S. dollar and a London pound [gold price], so we should have a price in China." The Chinese are aiming high. Their intention is not to simply be a major player in the gold markets, but to "become the world's leading marketplace for gold trading since the country produces and is holding the most gold reserves [in the world]," according to Shen Gang, the vice president of SGE in a recent CNBC interview. ("Shanghai shines brighter with 'Gold Exchange', http://english.cntv.cn/2015/07/17/ARTI1437116438830823.shtml (Accessed 08/26/2015))

In contrast, the COMEX gold market has become corrupt to the core. The banker cabal has suppressed the price of gold for years. The basic methods are to conduct naked shorting of the gold futures contract, selling paper gold, and failing to deliver on the naked shorts. Since June 2012, the gold futures contracts have been settled in cash only. No gold has been paid out since then. Curiously, the Commodities and Futures Trade Commission (CFTC) has not made a single complaint against this unlawful activity.

The Shanghai Gold Exchange has become the savior for the global economy by opening up the gold market to the world so that gold can truly be re-born as the anchor of the global monetary system. This is the sad truth of the global economy—that honest, hard-working people of the world look to China and the Shanghai Gold Exchange to create and maintain an honest market for gold and silver because the Western markets have become so utterly corrupt.

The Chinese have their own ratings agency that rival Standard & Poor's, Moody's and Fitch called Dagong Global which was founded in 1994 in Beijing. During the 2008 global financial crisis, Dagong took the opportunity to declare that the crisis was, in fact, caused by the Western financial institutions themselves including the Western ratings agencies. In their website, it states the following:

"In 2008, when people were shocked by the unexpected financial crisis, Dagong firstly revealed that the international credit rating system controlled by the largest debtor country is the origin of the crisis and made a proposal of building up a new international credit rating system. . . .Dagong has successfully undertaken the historic mission. . . It chooses the development road of internationalization as a national brand, that is to say, contribute the achievements made by Chinese in credit rating field to the world."
Guan Jianshong, President and CEO of Dagong Global Credit Rating Co., Ltd
September 16, 2012 (Wikipedia, "Dagong Global Credit Rating," https://en.wikipedia.org/wiki/Dagong_Global_Credit_Rating, (accessed September 8, 2015))

It is common knowledge in the United States that the rating agencies, Standard & Poors, Moody's and Fitch, are beholden to the big banks and rubber-stamp the opinions of the banker cabal. However, most Americans do not fully comprehend the extent to which the banker cabal, led by the Federal Reserve, actually dictates policy to the entire federal government of the United States. It must be emphasized that the Federal Reserve is a private banking cartel whose sole purpose is to make a profit for its shareholders. It is not a federal government institution as its deceptive name implies.

So it comes as no surprise that the Chinese have formed their own ratings agencies that may possibly be less corrupt than those of the United States. The level of corruption in Wall Street and in Washington, DC has become pervasive. Perhaps, the ethos of the American people has become more and more corrupt in parallel to the corruption at the highest levels of government. This may be why so few speak out against or even realize the degree of arrogance and greed within the United States government and its institutions.

The Chinese have their own credit card, China UnionPay or UnionPay, and it has become the second largest payment network by value of transactions processed, behind Visa. UnionPay cards can be used in 141 countries and regions around the world. UnionPay was founded on March 26, 2002 and is an association for China's banking card industry, operating under the approval of the People's Bank of China (PBOC, central bank of China).

UnionPay is also the only interbank network in China excluding Hong Kong and Macau, linking ATMs of all banks throughout mainland China and widely accepted by the ATMs in Hong Kong and Macau. It is also an EFTPOS (Electronic Funds Transfer at Point of Sale) network. (Wikipedia, "China UnionPay," https://en.wikipedia.org/wiki/China_UnionPay (Accessed September 8, 2015))

In the first quarter of 2015, China's UnionPay total transaction value exceeded US$1.9 trillion globally which means China UnionPay surpassed VISA for the first time in transaction value, becoming the biggest card liquidation organization in the world. According to the financial report of VISA, the total transaction value of VISA was US $1.75 trillion in the first quarter of 2015.

In total, UnionPay has issued some 5 billion cards in 40 countries, can be used in 150 countries and regions with over 26 million merchants and 1.8 million ATMs all over the world. (China Internet Watch, "China UnionPay Surpassed VISA in Transaction Value in Q1 2015," http://www.chinainternetwatch.com/13563 (accessed September 11, 2015))

In order to fully compete with the SWIFT global payments system of the West, China has created its own "alternative payments system which would provide a network that enables financial institutions worldwide to send and receive information about financial transactions in a secure, standardized and reliable environment." (Wikipedia, China International Payments System, https://en.wikipedia.org/wiki/China_International_Payments_System (accessed September 22, 2015))

According to the Washington Post, "CIPS is set to debut before the end of 2015 and has the potential to make the Chinese renminbi (RMB) or yuan a truly international, convertible currency and more attractive for conducting international trade and finance." As the world's second largest economy, it makes perfect sense that it would like to create its own international payments system and it has the wherewithal to do so. The renminbi or yuan accounts for nearly 9 percent of all trade finance deals worldwide, second only to the dollar. (Washington Post, The one Chinese innovation that could change the way we think about money, https://www.washingtonpost.com/news/innovations/wp/2015/03/10 (accessed September 22, 2015))

The RMB is now the fifth most used currency in the world, trailing only the dollar, the euro, the pound sterling, and the yen. This is "an important milestone" that confirms the transition of the renminbi from an "emerging" to a "business as usual" payment currency, according to Wim Raymaekers, Head of Banking Markets at SWIFT.

Now imagine Saudi Arabia pricing its oil in Yuan for the benefit of its largest customer, China. As the petrodollar is already being dismantled by the FOREX markets, this would open the floodgates to the rest of the world's oil-producing countries to price oil in currencies other than the dollar. Ultimately, the United States cannot point a gun at the head of the entire rest of the world because the rest of the world would then turn around and quarantine the United States. This scenario is one possible outcome of the ensuing "dollar implosion" which we are all now experiencing both in the United States and around the globe.

For More Information,
Please Visit www.DollarImplosion.com.

CHAPTER 8

DIGITAL GOLD—THE NEW GLOBAL CURRENCY

*In the midst of the economic chaos in the neighborhood, Chen (**China**), Ashish (**India**), and Carlos (**Brazil**) had a stroke of genius. They reasoned that in order for their new currency to be the victor in the "currency wars," it would have to be completely electronic—a digital currency. It would also have to be based on the amount of gold that each possessed so that nobody could merely create more currency out of thin air.*

These three young men had been accumulating gold for many years, so they figured they would have much to gain from this new currency. They created a new digital gold-based currency called the "dorado." They soon began using the "dorado" in transactions between themselves. This new currency was entirely digital meaning that no physical currency changed hands making this system of exchange much more efficient than Johnny's.

*Mohammed (**Tunisia**), Hassan (**Egypt**), Ali (**Libya**), Mehmet (**Turkey**), and Minjoon (**South Korea**) saw the writing on the wall. Johnny's dollar-based system was collapsing and they did not want to lose their hard-earned savings in the process. So these young men joined Chen, Ashish, and Carlos and began using the "dorado," as well. This* system worked well and soon the "dorado" was a major rival to the dollar.

Alexander (**Russia**) heard about the new gold-based currency and decided he, too, would join the rest of the young men in the neighborhood. He remembered the brutal fight he had gotten into with Karl many years ago and wanted revenge. Besides, he had accumulated a large amount of wealth through the meteoric success of his oil company and he wanted to make sure he kept it. With the mighty Alexander adopting the "dorado," there was no stopping the new, more efficient, digital gold-based currency.

Johnny was appalled by the incredible success of the new digital currency, the "dorado!" He never imagined there could be any rival to the dollar which he so ingeniously created. But he had a mountain of problems facing him and didn't have the time or energy to fight back. He was still in debt and was slowly working his way out of the situation. So he sat idly by as the younger men developed a whole new currency system. At least he had his friends Karl, Oliver and Nicholas, or so he thought.

Karl, Oliver and Nicholas watched with astonishment as the "dorado" became widely accepted and the dollar began to lose value like a sinking rock. Finally, they caved in and accepted the new currency, the "dorado." They did not want to be the ones holding the bag as the dollar imploded!

Johnny knew in his heart that the dollar was doomed. He had no choice but to accept the demise of the dollar and start his life anew. So he cashed in his last remaining assets for gold which he then used to buy "dorado" and join the rest of the guys in the neighborhood (**Digital global gold-based currency is created**). . .

If the dollar and other fiat currencies are doomed to fail in a few short years, what can we use to store wealth? The answer is gold and silver. Throughout human history, gold has held a special place as a store of wealth. Today, this still holds true. Gold can be bought in a number of forms: physical gold, gold-mining stocks, gold ETFs, precious metals mutual funds, and digital gold.

The economic and political exigencies of today are forcing us to develop a new global currency. But this trend is simply another step in the evolution of money itself. We humans have gone from utilizing barter, metal coins, paper money, paper checks, and electronic transactions, to eventually creating a digital global currency (DGC) which will likely be based on gold. Wikipedia defines digital gold currency in the following way:

> . . .*a form of electronic money based on ounces of gold. It is a kind of representative money, like a US paper gold certificate at the time (from 1873 to 1933) that these were exchangeable for gold on demand. The typical unit of account for such currency is the gold gram or the troy ounce, although other units such as the gold dinar are sometimes used. DGCs are backed by gold through unallocated or allocated gold storage.* (Wikipedia, "Digital Gold Currency" http://en.wikipedia.org/wiki/Digital_gold_currency (accessed February 16, 2012))

In fact, many U.S. states are beginning to issue their own currency. This practice will be attacked by the federal government; it will have no choice. If this practice were to become widespread, the federal government would risk losing control over the individual states, which it would never allow to happen.

According to James Turk and John Rubino, the authors of *The*

Collapse of the Dollar and How to Profit from It, the "digitization" of money is the solution to the world's currency problems:

> *If money is a means of communication, and Internet is the world's most powerful communications medium, then the Internet can allow gold to circulate as currency, making it once again the world's common language for economic calculation. Convert gold into bits, in other words, and you've retained all its strengths as money while eliminating its weaknesses as currency.* (Turk and Rubino 2004, 206)

Of course, one of the leading digital gold currencies is James Turk's "GoldMoney." Mr. Turk stands to gain immensely from this momentous shift in monetary exchange mediums. But ultimately, we will all benefit from a more stable system that is not exploited by the government and bankers to the detriment of the masses.

If digital gold currency becomes accepted, Turk and Rubino surmise that the value of gold will increase as the more people buy into the system. This is because when someone buys digital gold, the currency manager theoretically is storing gold away, thereby taking it out of circulation, increasing the demand for gold and incrementally raising gold's exchange rate. This is in contradistinction to what happens to paper currency when governments print more of it: the currency incrementally loses value because supply is increased.

This process will more rapidly increase the value of gold over the next several years. The theory is that the more people buy digital gold, the higher goes the price of gold, enticing even more people to buy gold, leading to the higher price of gold, in a positive feedback loop. Even those who do not possess extra capital to invest could still utilize digital gold-based currency for basic living expenses, similar to a checking account at a local bank. Eventually, the central bankers of the world's strongest economies will be forced to create or utilize a new global currency that cannot be manipulated by any one nation.

According to Wikipedia, the term "usury" refers to the charging of excessively high rates of interest. While the term "usury" originally meant the charging of any interest on loans, it acquired its modern connotation during Roman times.

During the decline of the Roman empire in the third century, the Romans endured currency devaluation, similar to what we are experiencing today in the United States. The rich Roman moneylenders charged exorbitantly high rates of interest to the peasant class, who were under ever-increasing tax demands and who were eventually reduced to serfdom. The term, usury, became synonymous with the exploitation of the poor.

The Catholic Church opposed the practice of usury because it meant that people would become excessively worried about money, thereby subjugating the God-given sanctity of life to man-made artificial notions of material wealth. The Catholic Church has consistently opposed usury throughout the centuries. Many edicts and laws were made condemning the practice by Christian clergy and lay people:

- *The First Council of Nicaea, in 325, forbade clergy from engaging in usury (canon 17). At the time, usury was interest of any kind, and the canon merely forbade the clergy to lend money on interest above 1 percent per month (12.7 percent APR). Later ecumenical councils applied this regulation to the laity.*
- *Lateran III decreed that persons who accepted interest on loans could receive neither the sacraments nor Christian burial.*
- *Pope Clement V made the belief in the right to usury a heresy in 1311, and abolished all secular legislation which allowed it.*
- *Pope Sixtus V condemned the practice of charging interest as "detestable to God and man, damned by the sacred canons and*

contrary to Christian charity." (Wikipedia, "Usury," http://en.wikipedia.org/wiki/Usury (accessed February 16, 2012))

Numerous other cultures and religions have stated the unjustness of the practice of usury as well. However, the Old Testament of the Bible apparently forbade the practice of charging interest between Jews, but allowed the practice when charged to non-Jews or foreigners.

- *Thou shalt not lend upon interest to thy brother: interest of money, interest of victuals, interest of anything that is lent upon interest (Holy Bible, Deuteronomy 23:19)*
- *Unto a foreigner thou mayest lend upon interest; but unto thy brother thou shalt not lend upon interest; that the LORD thy God may bless thee in all that thou puttest thy hand unto, in the land whither thou goest in to possess it. (Holy Bible, Deuteronomy 23:20)*

The historian Paul Johnson further asserts that since Jews were ostracized from most professions by local rulers, the church, and the guilds, they were pushed into marginal occupations at the time, such as tax and rent collecting and moneylending. The Jews, who were doing the "dirty work" of the ruling class, became even more disliked by the Roman people. Again, the Wikipedia article on usury describes the situation:

> *The Christians, on the basis of the Biblical rulings, condemned interest-taking absolutely, and from 1179 those who practiced it were excommunicated. Catholic autocrats frequently imposed the harshest financial burdens on the Jews. The Jews reacted by engaging in the one business where Christian laws actually discriminated in their favor, and became identified with the hated trade of moneylending. Peasants were*

forced to pay their taxes to Jews who were economically coerced into becoming the "front men" for the lords. The Jews would then be identified as the people taking their earnings. Meanwhile the peasants would remain loyal to the lords.
(Wikipedia, "Usury." http://en.wikipedia.org/wiki/ Usury (accessed March 20, 2012))

Interest of any kind is forbidden in Islam. As such, specialized codes of banking have developed to cater to investors wishing to obey Qur'anic law. Of course, most banks in the Muslim world do charge interest. Obviously, greed is a universal trait that is not exclusive to any religion or culture.

The new global electronic currency will lessen the problem of usury for humanity. This is because the playing field will be leveled. This means that interest rates will be the same for all those who utilize the same global currency. Individual nations' central banks will not be able to artificially raise or lower their interest rates based on their narrow economic goals. As a result, there should be less manipulation of interest rates for the benefit of wealthy individuals and corporations. The wealthy will still profit from charging interest on lending money, but the interest rate will be stable and reasonable.

It is the unreasonable interest rates charged by credit card companies, for instance, that lead to economic problems for the masses of people who utilize them. Similarly, the artificially high rates of interest charged by some banks when people cannot make payments on their loans will become more reasonable. Usury is probably the single biggest problem with the Western economic model and it will certainly need to be addressed by the creators of the new global digital currency.

THE INEXORABLE RISE OF GOLD AND SILVER

Gold has been a steady store of value for five thousand years. No paper (fiat) currency has stood the test of time—they have all become worthless. What's difficult to comprehend is that the U.S. dollar, the world's reserve currency, will also eventually become worthless. The entire world is waking up to the fact that the Almighty Dollar is imploding. The Chinese, Indians, Russians, Turks, and others around the world are buying more and more gold. Even Americans are slowly putting more and more of their wealth into gold.

Some analysts like Doug Casey assert that "gold is not only going through the roof, it is going to the moon." Mr. Casey is the editor of the newsletter, *International Speculator*, and author of the best-selling *Crisis Investing* and *The International Man*. David Morgan, editor of the precious metals newsletter, *The Morgan Report*, states that the incredible rise in the price of gold in the 1970s was just a prelude to what is going to happen to the price of gold this time around.

Simply stated, the more the dollar loses value, the higher goes the price of gold. No one knows for sure how high the price of gold will go, but some experts such as Jim Rickards predict $10,000 per ounce by 2020! Rickards has authored such books as Currency Wars, The Death of Money and The New Case for Gold and has a long and storied career both in the private sector and in the government. In fact, Rickards makes a strong case that the world has simply rewritten the "rules of the game" at least 3 times in the past 100 years—in 1914, 1939 and 1971.

Rickards argues that U.S. President Donald Trump may have the power and vision to convene the "Mar-A-Lago Accord" in which the world's most powerful financial actors meet at his retreat in Mar-A-Lago, Florida to rewrite the rules of the international finance and effectively revalue the price of gold to $10,000 per ounce. He uses mathematical analysis to arrive at the figure of $10,000 per ounce based on the amount of gold in existence and the global money supply. He even suggests that the world's fiat currencies would be *revalued* according to the actual amount of gold that each country's central bank possesses.

Silver follows gold as a store of value, but it is more volatile. If gold is like a 747 airliner, silver would be a fighter jet. Perhaps the upside of silver is potentially even higher than gold. According to Jim Rickards, when the dollar value of gold is set at $10,000 per ounce, the corresponding value of silver should be roughly $400 per ounce. Certainly, those investors who wish to profit from the current rise in the price of gold and silver may wish to benefit from the increased volatility of silver compared to gold.

In other words, both gold and silver will continue to rise in price for the rest of the decade, but gold is a more conservative investment while silver is a more aggressive investment. The average investor can't lose either way, or with a combination of both. More adventurous investors can take advantage of the volatility of silver, knowing that the overall trend in the price of silver is up for the next several years. In other words, buy silver on margin at the "trough" and sell it at the "peak." Take profits. Wait for the price of silver to go down and repeat the entire process. This is a surefire method of profiting from the rather volatile rise in the price of silver for the rest of the decade.

- **Pay off credit card debt**.
- **Change your adjustable rate mortgage to fixed rate mortgage**.
- **Speculate on the falling dollar**:
(1) Short-term speculation: Dollar Index put options, Euro call options
(2) Long-term speculation: Foreign Currency Certificates of Deposit

- **Buy gold and silver!**
(1) Buy gold bullion: You can either have the bullion shipped to your home or have it stored for you. The oldest and most reputable precious metals company based in the United States is **Monex**, based in Newport Beach, California. Other very reputable gold bullion companies are **BullionVault**, based in London, and **GoldMoney**, based in Jersey which is a sovereign country located in the English Channel. Jim Rickards has specifically recommended the **PMC Ounce from Neptune-GBX Global Bullion Exchange**. (The PMC Ounce is a fixed quantity of gold, silver, palladium and platinum that has a real-time spot market price and offers investors the option to convert their holdings of PMC Ounces into metal for delivery.)
(2) Buy gold exchange-traded funds: An ETF is a type of mutual fund that trades like a stock and tracks the price of gold. "**GLD**" (for streetTRACKS Gold Trust) and "**IAU**" (for the iShares COMEX Gold Trust) are the two choices here.
(3) Buy gold mutual funds, stocks, and gold futures and options: All of these require further in-depth knowledge of the individual gold mining companies. This option is for the seasoned stock trader.

I personally believe that buying gold or silver bullion directly is the safest method of protecting your wealth. You do not have to store the gold yourself. You can even open an account overseas with an international gold bullion dealer like BullionVault and have your wealth stored safely beyond the greedy clutches of the United States government. Generationally wealthy investors love this option the most.

As more and more Americans pull their dollars out of banks and buy non-dollar-based assets such as gold, silver, foreign currencies, and foreign real estate, the banking industry will suffer. Not only will banks fail, but so will much of the financial services sector, including investment banks and insurance companies. This may seem like an outlandish prediction, but it is bound to happen.

The only people who consistently make money in the stock market are those in the industry. They make money on commissions and fees, regardless of what happens in the markets. But they will lose if we collectively take our money and put it into hard assets like gold and silver.

We are now at the beginning of this huge sea change in financial thinking. More and more individuals are buying more and more gold and silver in the United States. Signs are springing up around the United States, "Will buy your gold!" and "Sell your gold jewelry for best price!" Around the world, the Chinese and Indian governments are buying more gold and less U.S. Treasuries. Meanwhile, the Chinese and Indian people are continuing to put their wealth into gold.

So it behooves us all to take action now or risk losing our entire life savings. Remember, the government and the financial services industry both wish to see us lose our life savings to inflation, because they benefit disproportionately from inflation. Those of us who see the big picture are now refusing to allow our savings to be wiped out by inflation. We are putting our money into gold and silver by the droves.

Thus, the American government will be forced to abandon the

"Almighty Dollar" and to help create a sound, globally integrated financial system. The current international banking system will be forever transformed and the American empire will shrink. This is how we Americans will finally pay for the debt which we have accumulated over history, the vast majority of which we have accumulated in the last forty years.

You must act quickly because time is running out fast before the dollar collapses and gold and silver explode. The pace of change in the global financial system is accelerating toward the inevitable global financial reset. Now is the time to hedge your bets by buying gold and silver bars and coins and opening up gold and silver accounts with Apmex, BullionVault, GoldMoney, Monex, Neptune-GBX or any other reputable company.

Who will be the big losers when the dollar implodes? The biggest losers will be the entities that profit from the dollar currently—Wall Street and the United States government. They will lose more and more of the hard-earned dollars of the average American, as gold and silver become more and more popular investment vehicles for the masses. Wall Street doesn't make any money when the average investor shifts his or her portfolio toward gold and silver.

As for the average American, he will suffer throughout the entire process of dollar collapse by bearing the brunt of the triple-whammy of rising inflation, interest rates and unemployment. In fact, the ultimate collapse of the dollar and subsequent bursting of the government debt bubble will actually be a greeted with a sigh of relief by the masses. This is because the United States government will be forced to end its policy of money-printing thereby halting or significantly slowing down the rate of rise of inflation.

The old investment adage of diversification into stocks, bonds, mutual funds, and gold has become outdated. The new investment strategy is "***Concentrate the bulk of your portfolio in gold and silver and enjoy the ride through the end of the decade and beyond.***" You must go against the advice of the financial advisors and the financial establishment. Remember, when you shift your assets from cash, stocks, and bonds to gold, silver and commodities, their loss is your gain. They stand to lose money while you stand to gain.

It is true that gold is the ultimate bubble, and it will eventually pop, too. So when should you get out of gold and silver? When everybody including the shoeshine boy is saying to put your money into gold, then you know that the bubble will soon pop. We will not see this great event until the dollar bubble and the government bubble pop and there is a new international gold-based electronic currency on the horizon.

In the meantime, all people around the world who are still heavily invested in paper assets such as stocks, bonds, and mutual funds should begin to concentrate their wealth into gold, silver and other tangible assets. Perhaps a step-by-step plan of selling some stocks, bonds, and mutual funds and of buying gold and silver with the proceeds is an attractive method of shifting wealth into gold and silver.

Those who reallocate their wealth into gold, silver, and commodities will be protecting their wealth for generations to come. They will welcome the transition from the current fiat currency regime, with the U.S. dollar as the world's reserve currency, to a new international standard based on gold. They will have most of their wealth stored in gold and silver, and will continue to profit from the current upheaval by regularly converting their currency to gold and silver.

For More Information,
Please Visit www.DollarImplosion.com.

CHAPTER 9

NEW WORLD ORDER

*No longer was Johnny the strongest man in town. He no longer made the rules by which the other men in the neighborhood abided. He could hold his own, but could not dictate to others as he had done in the past. The strongest man on each block ruled that block. The neighborhood had become divided into miniature fiefdoms (**Regional Spheres of Influence**). Each block had a neighborhood watchman assigned for the night. So the men on each block took turns patrolling their block.*

*This drastically reduced Johnny's burden of having to patrol the entire neighborhood on his own (**United States relinquishes role of global policeman**). He now had much more time to deal with his financial issues. But he was still dependent on his ex-wife to take care of his children (**America still dependent on Saudi Arabian oil**). He knew that once his children reached the age of emancipation, he would no longer be dependent on her. Regardless, he loved his children and would do anything possible for them.*

*Johnny's neighborhood looked much different now than when Johnny was in his prime. Mohammed (**Tunisia**), Hassan (**Egypt**), and Ali (**Libya**) were now coming of age and they began building their own homes and standing up for themselves in neighborhood affairs. They were becoming wealthier, too, now that the entire neighborhood began using the new gold-based currency.*

No longer could Johnny print as many dollars as he wished. The dollar-based system served the neighborhood well for some time, but it was time to evolve to a more equitable financial system whereby all could benefit, not just the already wealthy individuals—Johnny, Oliver, Karl and Nicholas.

The new, more balanced power structure and financial system not only lessened the burden on Johnny--it also forced the others to participate and contribute to the new neighborhood watch program. The boys had grown up to become strong young men and contribute to the security and wellbeing of the neighborhood.

*Everyone pulled their own weight rather than relying on Johnny to save the day whenever there was a skirmish in the neighborhood. This new system seemed to work much more efficiently and equitably for all (**Multipolar geopolitical system is created**).*

The World Bank apparently took notice of the shifting dynamics in the global power structure which was dominated by the United States after winning the Cold War. In 2011, it published an analysis of the new world economic order entitled *Multipolarity: The New Global Economy*. In this erudite analysis of the global economic changes, the authors state the following:

> *Sweeping changes are afoot in the global economy. As the second decade of the 21st century unfolds and the world exits from the 2008-09 financial crisis, the growing clout of emerging markets is paving the way for a world economy with an increasingly multipolar character. The distribution of global growth will become more diffuse, with no single country dominating the global economic scene.* (World Bank, "Multipolarity: The New Global Economy," 2011, 1)

They go on to state that the developing countries' share of international trade flows have increased from 30 percent in 1995 to 45 percent in 2010. They also state that developing and emerging countries now hold two-thirds of the world's foreign exchange reserves, roughly $6 trillion of the total foreign reserves of $9 trillion, with China holding a whopping $3 trillion itself.

After much detailed analysis, the authors of the World Bank report pose three different scenarios for the period of 2011 to 2025:

(1) *Dollar standard remains the status quo: the U.S. dollar remains the world's reserve currency.*

(2) *Multipolar international currencies: the dollar loses its position as the dominant international currency to be replaced by a global system including three equally important currencies, the dollar, the euro, and an Asian currency.*

(3) *New single multilateral reserve currency: the major economic powers led by the United States forge a new international currency managed by a global central bank.*
(World Bank, "Multipolarity: The New Global Economy," 2011, 144-5)

Interestingly, the authors state that given current trends, the second scenario of multipolar international currencies is most likely to play out. The report goes on to assert the single multilateral reserve currency is far less likely than the other two scenarios to materialize over the next fifteen years, as "the multilateral reserve scenario would necessitate developing a set of rules for managing international liquidity and moderating exchange rate movements and would require countries highly protective of their national monetary policy to relinquish full control." (World Bank, "Multipolarity: The New Global Economy," 2011, 145-6)

However, the World Bank report does not mention the huge debt burden of the United States; nor does it mention the contraction of the United States economy. The fundamentals point to an unsustainable economic situation for the United States of America. As a result, the World Bank report fails to recognize the inevitable dollar implosion, the rapid collapse in the value of the dollar which will likely take place in the latter half of this decade.

Just as the World Bank, International Monetary Fund, and other major financial institutions did not predict the financial crisis of 2008–09, the authors of this World Bank report fail to see the imminent collapse of the dollar. They fail to recognize the dollar bubble and the mechanics of economic bubbles. **Bubbles do not simply deflate slowly—they pop!**

The imminent dollar collapse will ultimately force the hand of the United States government to acquiesce to a new international reserve currency—**the International Monetary Fund's SDR (Standard Drawing Rights)**. The SDR already exists as a possible alternative to the dollar as the global reserve currency. However, it is only recently that a new technology based on blockchains called **Distributed Ledger Technology** can be implemented to make the SDR the global reserve currency. This would *not* mean that people would walk around with SDR's in their pockets. Rather, the world's central banks would simply use SDRs more so than the U.S. Dollar, Euro, Yen, Pound Sterling, Swiss Franc or Chinese Yuan as a store of value and to settle balance of trade issues.

But the politicians will resort to blowing the last bubble left in their armamentarium, the government debt bubble. They may continue to blow this bubble for several more years before the bubble bursts. Then it will be "game over" for the American empire. The global currency reset will be implemented by the world's major economic powers. Given the powerful historical and economic forces at play, this is the most likely scenario to play out in the future.

The European Union, Japan and China will also benefit from the formation of a new global currency reset, because they are also enduring major currency and trade imbalances, which are causing problems for their economies. It may take failed attempts, at first, but ultimately there will be a global currency reset based on the newly agreed upon gold standard.

In other words, we will live in a multipolar world with a single global electronic currency. In the new world order, no single country will possess the world's reserve currency. Therefore, no single country will be able to finance huge unsustainable levels of debt. The imbalances created by politicians in government will be a thing of the past. Politicians will have to run on realistic platforms. Governments will be forced to live within their means. This means that governments will have to spend roughly what they collect in revenue.

This is a revolutionary concept because governments around the world have become quite accustomed to printing money. All governments benefit from the ability to print money. They not only manipulate the interest rates to their benefit. They also print money and loan it to themselves when they need it, thereby shifting the burden of the debt to future generations.

Can the American empire survive without the benefit of having the world's reserve currency? The answer is "No, not in its current form." The American empire will have to shrink dramatically. A large percentage of its overseas military bases will have to be shut down, because the defense budget will be massively decreased. The Medicare budget will be slashed and Medicaid will be the *de facto* healthcare plan for all who cannot afford to pay for health insurance. Social Security will be reduced to a need-only basis.

This will be the first time in history that the world's major economies will be financially reliant on one another. There will be a higher order of financial integration between the world's nations and their economies. The Internet and global telecommunications have already created an electromagnetic nervous system for the entire planet, which has evolved from radio and television.

Taking into account these globalization trends, it makes perfect sense that humanity will soon evolve to a single, global medium of exchange based on relative quantities of gold possessed by each country. The world's brilliantly diverse cultures will be forced to live peacefully with one another. This will be a truly exciting time to be alive! Is there any other evidence or body of knowledge to support the idea of a new financial world order or new world order in general? Yes. The world's diverse religious and cultural traditions offer compelling prophesies for the "end of time" and a paradigm shift to a more enlightened human civilization—a **new world order**.

Many cultures and traditions foretell the "end of time." For example, in the United States, the Judeo-Christian tradition is based on the Bible, both the Old and New Testaments. The Book of Mark tells of a time of great upheaval, when those who have sinned will fall from grace and the Earth will witness the second coming of Jesus Christ in the Apocalypse.

However, the Apocalypse is only the beginning of the end. According to the Book of Revelation, it will be followed by a final battle at the end, the final judgment, and a heavenly Jerusalem:

> *Then the One sitting on the throne spoke: "Now I am making the whole of creation new," he said. "Write this: that what I am saying is sure and will come true." And then he said, "It is already done. I am the Alpha and the Omega, the Beginning and the End. I will give water from the well of life free to anybody who is thirsty; it is the rightful inheritance of the one who proves victorious; and I will be his God and he is a son to me. But the legacy for cowards, for those who break their word, or worship obscenities, for murderers and fornicators, and for fortunetellers, idolaters, or any other sort of liars, is the second death in the burning lake of sulphur.*
> (Holy Bible, Revelation 21:1-8)

This prophecy is astounding. It clearly foresees a time of great upheaval for humanity, followed by the righteous being saved while the sinners go to Hell. Many theologians and historians alike believe that humanity is actually living through this time of great upheaval and transformation, early in the twenty-first century. One Christian pastor even predicted that May 21, 2011 would be the end of the world. But perhaps the end of the world is meant figuratively, not literally. Perhaps, biblical prophecy refers to the paradigm shift from the materialistic Industrial Age to the more balanced **Age of the Individual**.

According to Wikipedia, "Shemitah or Shmita is the Sabbath year, sabbatical year or seventh year of the seven-year agricultural cycle mandated by the Torah for the Land of Israel, and still observed in contemporary Judaism." During shmita, the land is left to lie fallow and all plowing, planting, pruning and harvesting is forbidden by halakha (Jewish law). Wikipedia, "Shmita," https://en.wikipedia. org/wiki/Shmita (accessed September 14, 2015))

A Sabbath or shemitah year is mentioned several times in the Bible by name or by its pattern of six years of activity and one of rest. Here are just of few of those Biblical references:

- Book of Exodus: "You may plant your land for six years and gather its crops. But during the seventh year, you must leave it alone and withdraw from it. The needy among you will then be able to eat just as you do, and whatever is left over can be eaten by wild animals. This also applies to your vineyard and your olive grove." (Exodus 23: 10-11)
- Book of Leviticus: "God spoke to Moses at Mount Sinai, telling him to speak to the Israelites and say to them: When you come to the land that I am giving you, the land must be given a rest period, a Sabbath to God. For six years you may plant your fields, prune your vineyards, and harvest your crops, but the seventh year is a Sabbath of Sabbaths for the land. It is God's Sabbath during which you may not plant your fields, nor prune your vineyards. Do not harvest crops that grow on their own and do not gather the grapes on your unpruned vines, since it is a year of rest for the land. . . (Leviticus 25: 1-7)
- Book of Deuteronomy: "At the end of every seven years, you shall celebrate the remission year. The idea of the remission year is that every creditor shall remit any debt owed by his

neighbor and brother when God's remission year comes around. You may collect from the alien, but if you have any claim against your brother for a debt, you must relinquish it. . . (Deuteronomy 15: 1-6)

For the modern State of Israel, the first Shemitah year was 1951-52, followed by 1958-59, 1965-66, 1972-73, 1979-80, 1986-87, 1993-94, 2000-01, 2007-08, 2014-15. The most recent Shemitah year began in September 2014 and ended on September 13, 2015. These Shemitah years are a time of "shaking" of the current system and subsequent renewal. During the last two cycles, we witnessed historic stock market crashes on the very last day of the Shemitah year.

For example, on September 17, 2001, we witnessed the greatest one-day stock market crash in all of U.S. history up until that time. The Dow plunged 684 points, and it was a record that held for exactly seven years until the end of the next Shemitah cycle. On September 29, 2008, the Dow plummeted 777 points, which still today remains the greatest one-day stock market crash of all time in the United States.

According to Muslims, the Qur'an is not myth for Muslims; it is the actual word of Allah. Nevertheless, it is very similar to the Bible in its description of the end of times. It describes a time of natural catastrophes on Earth, followed by the division of people into the blessed, the damned, and the truly holy ones:

> *When the earth shakes and quivers and the mountains crumble away and scatter into fine dust, you shall be divided into three multitudes: those on the right (blessed shall be those on the right!); those of the left (damned shall be those on the left!); and those to the fore (foremost shall be those!). Such are they that shall be brought near to their Lord in the gardens of delight: a whole multitude from the men of old, but only a few from the later generations.*
> (Qu'ran, "al-Qiyamah," 75th Sura)

The Book of Hadith, a collection of oral traditions attributed to the Prophet Muhammad, tells the story of the end of the world in striking detail. It tells of a time when people will no longer study the Qur'an, but will spend their time seeking pleasure, material wealth and worldly power. There will be earthquakes, famines, epidemics, and floods. The morality that binds together human society will disintegrate, and it will be every man for himself. Dajjal, the Antichrist, will rule supreme over the earth. Then Jesus will come down from the heavens on a white horse and slay the evil Dajjal.

Jesus will then reign over the earth for eighty-seven years. After his reign, he will go to Jerusalem and pray at the Mosque of the Dome of the Rock. God will then take Jesus into heaven. The monsters, Gog and Magog, will break free and wreak havoc on earth. God will then summon two angels into service. Azrail, the angel of death, will appear as a star to the believers and as a monster to the non-believers. Then the angel Israfil will blow his mighty trumpet three times. At the third blast of the trumpet, the prophet Muhammad will return to earth on his horse, Burak, led by the angel Gabriel:

> *The throne of God will then be visible to all. There will be no secrets: The secret sins of everyone, believer and unbeliever, will be known to all. These secret sins will be weighed on the left side of the scale, and all good deeds, no matter how small, will be weighed on the right. If the right outweighs the left, then the soul is saved; if the opposite is true, the soul will be damned. (Book of Hadith, Book 84, Hadith 69)*

Jose Arguelles, PhD, author of *The Mayan Factor* (1987) first popularized the concept of the Mayan calendar. In that book, he concluded that "the Mayan calendar system was not meant to measure time but to record the harmonic calibrations of a galactic synchronization beam, 5,125-years or 5200-tun (360-day cycles) in duration. According to the time science of the ancient Maya, a great moment of transformation awaits us at 2012, when we pass out of that beam." (Arguelles 1987, 9-10)

Dr. Arguelles further asserts that, according to the Mayans, humanity will pass into a post-historic, galactic phase of evolution. He discusses the concept that we will think and act as a single planetary organism. He concludes, "With the advent of planetary consciousness will come, not destruction, but, at long last, universal peace."

The Mayans were somehow able to map out the evolution of humanity and planet earth with amazing precision. This Mayan prophecy has made its way into popular American culture with the release of the science fiction disaster film "2012" (starring John Cusack, Woody Harrelson, and others), depicting cataclysmic events.

In essence, all the world's religions and cultures have all foretold a time of upheaval and transformation. Humanity does sense the transformation taking place. Perhaps the dollar implosion we are experiencing is simply part of a larger global transformation to a higher level of planetary integration. The world's religions and cultures have certainly foretold a time of great transformation. Perhaps that time is now.

For More Information,
Please Visit www.DollarImplosion.com.

ACT IV
AGE OF THE INDIVIDUAL

CHAPTER 10

MASTERS OF OUR OWN DESTINY

Not only was the power structure and financial system in Johnny's neighborhood changing, so were the lives of the residents of the neighborhood. As part of getting his life on better footing, Johnny began to exercise regularly, eat healthy balanced meals and even took up yoga.

He realized that material wealth was only part of living a balanced life. He began to develop an inner happiness that did not depend on material riches. He became more resolute in strengthening the power of his mind. His life became more joyful as a result.

Johnny fervently believed in promoting health and wellness for himself and for the whole neighborhood. He felt so strongly about helping others live a healthy lifestyle that he started a new business devoted to health called "Johnny's Health & Wellness Superstore."

His new store became a one-stop shop for all of the neighborhood residents' health needs, from health books, magazines, and CD's to vitamins and diet supplements and even had computerized directories of health and wellness coaches. His new health store became wildly successful and Johnny became known far and wide as "Mr. Health and Wellness."

*Johnny had become good friends with his old nemesis, Hiroto (**Japan**), and with Minjoon (**South Korea**), as well. The middle-aged, wealthy men in the neighborhood (**G7 Industrialized Nations**)* *even decided to form a larger, more inclusive country club (**G20 Nations**) so that Chen (**China**), Carlos (**Brazil**), Ashish (**India**), Mehmet (**Turkey**), and the younger men in the neighborhood could play tennis and golf with the older men. The old system of street fighting to claim superiority over another was replaced by a more healthy system of competitive sports at the country club.*

*There were, of course, younger boys in the neighborhood who challenged the stronger men and received a good walloping from time to time. But eventually each and every man in the neighborhood could join the country club, if he played by the new rules. Karl (**Germany**), Oliver (**England**), and Nicholas (**France**) got into shape, too. They spent much time at the club exercising and playing tennis. They had not played tennis since their school years but were proving to be quite a match for the younger men in the club.*

*Mohammed (**Tunisia**), Hassan (**Egypt**) and Ali (**Libya**) each developed his own green energy company and they became wealthy in the process. Everybody who came of age in the neighborhood developed his strengths which helped the entire neighborhood prosper. They also joined the neighborhood country club and started the tradition of weekly soccer matches at the club. Chen and Hiroto were well-versed in the martial arts and offered lessons to the club members. Ashish and Malik (**Pakistan**) introduced the sport of cricket to the club.*

*Each and every individual in the neighborhood had the opportunity to develop himself to his fullest potential and to join the country club. The old system of "might makes right" had given way to a new, more equitable system based on the inherent value of each individual. Johnny's neighborhood had become a more civilized, peaceful, and vibrant place to live. It had become a "**heaven on earth**."*

INTERNET—THE GREAT EQUALIZER

The creation of the Internet by the U.S. government in 1969 has forever electronically linked the globe. It is the ever-increasing speed of information exchange that defines the Information Age--the Age of the Individual. But it is crucial for us to understand that faster and faster information exchange via technology is mirrored in our brains by higher levels of consciousness. Therefore, we as individuals and collectively as the human race must process and integrate ever increasing amounts of information into our individual and collective consciousness.

We search for larger and more inclusive worldviews to explain the world's events and we are left with a truly global perspective. This means that we must look at ourselves on planet earth as a global family. Just as families have unending quarrels between members, we have unending quarrels between countries. Yes, we can annihilate each other with nuclear weapons, just as family members occasionally resolve conflicts by killing each other. But we know that this is not the best way of solving conflicts around the world.

One global framework we may utilize is called the *Gaia Hypothesis*—the idea that the Earth and all of its creatures form one living organism. So, in essence, all of our technology is merely the development of the Earth's nervous system. With computers and the Internet, an individual can interact with other entities around the globe almost instantaneously. Governments around the world are still trying to control the Internet, but the process cannot be stopped.

The Internet is the true democratizing force in the world. It allows us to obtain information without it being filtered through an intermediary, as is the case with other forms of mass communication like radio and television. The linking up of millions of computers around the world is creating a larger organic entity known as cyberspace. Cyberspace is our global psyche and is what unifies the human race, simultaneously forming and shaping our global consciousness.

Governments around the world are trying to curtail the powerful democratizing force of the Internet. In 2011, the U.S. government recently went after the founder of WikiLeaks, Julian Assange, and had him arrested in Sweden for a bogus sex charge. But the real reason for his arrest is the embarrassment he caused the government by making public thousands of communiqués from government officials. WikiLeaks is a great example of the power of mass collaboration using the Internet.

In January 2012, the politicians in Washington, DC tried to pass landmark legislation designed to curtail the freedom of the Internet, the Stop Online Piracy Act (SOPA) and Protect IP Act (PIPA). This legislation was brought forth at the behest of large institutions such as the Recording Industry Association of America in an effort to protect their economic interest.

Opponents to the proposed legislation stated that this legislation would threaten free speech on the Internet and that the government could block access to entire internet domains. They also "raised concerns that SOPA would bypass the "safe harbor" protections from liability presently afforded to Internet sites by the Digital Millenium Copyright Act." (Wikipedia, "Stop Online Piracy Act," http://en.wikipedia.org/wiki/Stop_Online_Piracy_Act (accessed March 15, 2012))

On January 18, 2012, Wikipedia and thousands of other Internet sites coordinated a service "blackout" in protest of SOPA and PIPA. Google blacked out its famous name on its website in deference to the protest. Sure enough, the politicians in Washington got the message loud and clear and rescinded the proposed legislation.

In July 2012, individuals and organizations became so concerned about the efforts of the government and big business to control the Internet that they created the Declaration of Internet Freedom. The crux of this document is as follows:

"We stand for a free and open Internet. We support transparent and participatory processes for making Internet policy and the establishment of five basic principles:

- *Expression: Don't censor the Internet.*
- *Access: Promote universal access to fast and affordable networks.*
- *Openness: Keep the Internet an open network where everyone is free to connect, communicate, write, read, watch, speak, listen, learn, create and innovate.*
- *Innovation: Protect the freedom to innovate and create without permission. Don't block new technologies, and don't punish innovators for their users' actions.*
- *Privacy: Protect privacy and defend everyone's ability to control how their data and devices are used."*

(Yahoo News, "Internet lines up behind the Declaration of Internet Freedom, Fox Van Allen, http://news.yahoo.com/blogs/technology-blog/internet-lines-behind-declaration-internet-freedom-221654205.html (accessed July 2, 2012))

We are now entering the next phase of the Internet, the phase of mass collaboration. In the past, collaboration was relatively small-scale as used during anti-globalization rallies in Seattle and Washington, for example. Now individuals are linking up in networks of peers to produce goods and services, thereby shaping a new reality. Another name for mass collaboration is peer production. The most popular examples of successful peer production ventures include YouTube, Linux, and Wikipedia.

Large corporations are now using mass collaboration to build their products. For example, Boeing's 787 Dreamliner is a wonderful showcase of mass collaboration. In the post-9/11 world of higher fuel prices and more regulations, Boeing has had to rethink its way of doing business. Rather than the old, hierarchical method of Boeing designing the product from scratch and submitting the specifications to its suppliers, it has opened up the entire process of design and manufacturing to its suppliers.

This may seem like a Herculean task, to integrate all of these diverse and globally distributed designers and manufacturers into a highly complex project. But underlying this process is a real-time collaboration system created by Boeing and Dassault Systemes, linking all of the various partners via a single platform of management tools and data. Thus, any member of any team anywhere in the world can access, review, and contribute to the work-in-progress in real time. (Tapscott and Williams 2008, 224–30)

The final product, the 787 Dreamliner, was created by over one hundred suppliers from six countries. In fact, the authors of *Wikinomics*, Don Tapscott and Anthony D. Williams, go so far as to assert that the new paradigm of mass collaboration will be the ultimate engine of economic growth.

But when they use the term "mass collaboration," they are referring to the "ability to integrate the talents of dispersed individuals and organizations as becoming the defining competency for managers and firms." This fits beautifully with the notion of an increasingly linked network of human interaction worldwide via technological devices including the Internet, telephones, television, and global trade.

It is high time that individual human beings take control of their lives and become masters of their destiny. We all must decide if we want security or liberty. When we choose the security of larger and larger government, we give up our most precious gift in the world—freedom. This battle between security and freedom rages on today. The government and those who benefit from it want us to choose the safety and comfort of "Big Brother" over individual freedom and liberty.

We need look no further than the Declaration of Independence of the United States of America written on July 4, 1776 to impress upon ourselves the delicate balance of freedom and liberty for all human beings and the power of government to secure those rights:

"We hold these truths to be self-evident, that all men are created equal, that they are endowed by their Creator with certain unalienable Rights, that among these are Life, Liberty, and pursuit of Happiness.

--That to secure these rights, Governments are instituted among Men, deriving their just powers from the consent of the governed.

--That whenever any Form of Government becomes destructive of these ends, it is the Right of the People to alter or to abolish it, and to institute new Government, laying its foundation on such principles and organizing its powers in such form, as to them shall seem most likely to affect their Safety and Happiness."

As a society, we have become complacent and, as a result, we keep choosing the safety of larger and larger government. But our individual freedoms have been eroded in the process. The United States government now oversees every aspect of our lives, including our health and our personal finances. We must fight for our rights as individuals against the government. We are funding this massive increase in the size of our government by the people we put in power.

In fact, the size of the United States government has been steadily increasing since 2000 under both the Republican Bush administration and the Democratic Obama administration. Whereas the size of the government in the European Union has fairly consistently remained around 45 percent of GDP, the United States has seen the size of its government increase from roughly 30 percent of GDP in 2001 to 40 percent of GDP in 2009.

Perhaps the only good that will come of this increase in the size of government will paradoxically be the more rapid acceleration of its own demise. This is why we will see the United States dollar implode very soon. Then, once the dollar collapses, the U.S. government will default on its debt obligations and will be forced to make spending cuts across the board and to increase taxes as well. Only when the United States government drastically downsizes will Americans paradoxically regain their freedom!

WINDS OF CHANGE IN AMERICAN POLITICS

The rise of the Tea Party movement in the United States in 2009 exemplifies the winds of change in American politics. The name, Tea Party, refers to the Boston Tea Party in 1773 when the American colonists rebelled against "taxation without representation" by dumping British tea into the ocean. This influential movement is seen as both conservative and libertarian in ideology and grew out of the generalized disillusionment with politicians and government in 2009.

The Tea Party movement "endorses reduced government spending, reduction in taxation, reduction of the national debt and federal budget deficit and adherence to an originalist interpretation of the United States Constitution." In 2010, a massive wave of Tea Partiers were elected to state and federal government, but were hastily incorporated into the larger, more powerful Republican Party. (Wikipedia, "Tea Party movement." http://en.wikipedia.org/wiki/Tea_Party_movement, (accessed March 18, 2012))

The American political system is essentially a two-party system. Third parties have been attempted by such powerful figures as Ross Perot and others, but have not succeeded. One of the reasons is the tremendous political power of the two dominant political parties in the United States, the Republican and Democratic Parties.

However, the truth is that the independent voters in the United States have determined the outcome of elections in the United States, because the conservative Republican vote essentially cancels out the more liberal Democratic vote. The Occupy movement which was discussed earlier is another recent influential movement in the United States and abroad. In the span of a few months, this movement began to shape the tone and substance of political discourse. The Occupy movement has been criticized for lack of focus and leadership, but has been effective at utilizing the principle of non-violent sit-ins and demonstrations to draw attention to their issues of concern.

Another movement making great strides in American politics is Libertarianism. The Libertarian platform is basically conservative on financial issues and liberal on social issues. Jesse Ventura, the former governor of Minnesota, was elected on such a platform, but it did not catch on nationally.

Ron Paul, congressman from Texas, comes close to embodying the principles of the Libertarian philosophy and enjoys great support among the college campuses and independent voters. However, his support has not reached critical mass in the 2012 Republican Primary race to become a viable force in American politics (as of this writing). Interestingly, Ron Paul boasts the greatest support from young voters in their 20s and 30s, perhaps because this younger generation has the most to lose from continuing the current policies of deficit spending and ever-rising national debt.

One important aspect of Libertarian philosophy is the freedom to live one's life without government interference. This includes the use of recreational drugs, as long as it does not harm others. Perhaps the United States is ready for the legalization of soft drugs, especially in view of the fact that drug use has not declined in the United States as a result of the "war on drugs."

A major report in 2011 concluded that the war on drugs that was first started by President Nixon has failed. It has failed in curbing the use of drugs and in the trafficking of drugs. It also wastes billions of dollars of federal money in drug enforcement efforts. In addition, billions each year are spent on prosecuting drug cases in the U.S. courts.

Similarly, we are witnessing the gradual acceptance of the homosexual community throughout the United States. Many states have legalized gay marriage. In September 2011, the United States military passed an historic milestone with the repeal of the ban on gays serving openly in uniform, the so-called "Don't Ask, Don't Tell" policy. The United States military now openly allows homosexuals to serve in the armed forces. In June 2011, the United Nations for the first time in its history declared that gays and lesbians are entitled to the same rights as all human beings. (United Nations Declaration on Sexual Orientation and Gender Identity, New York, June 17, 2011)

In essence, the Tea Party movement, Occupy movement, and the resurgence of the Libertarian Party are all advocating severe limitation of the size and scope of government. This is a complete reversal of the trend toward larger and larger government since the birth of the American empire.

The main political parties in the United States, the Democratic and Republican parties, and the United States government itself, have a vested interest in maintaining the status quo. This explains the inherent conflict between these progressive populist movements and the entrenched political system.

Globalization, the Internet, technological advances, mass uprisings against dictators in the Middle East, and the evolutionary trend toward a global currency all empower the individual. It is high time that we all become masters of our own destiny! We have all of the tools at our disposal to choose freedom over a false sense of security. This means that we must not choose politicians who promise the world in return for putting future generations in debt. We must embrace a more libertarian philosophy as a people.

First of all, we must see the reality of the situation. All of the paper wealth in which we have believed is an illusion. It is illusory because it can be manipulated by other people. The stock market can be manipulated by large players and insider trading, thereby cheating the small investor of real earnings.

The U.S. dollar is being devalued at a dizzying rate by the federal government, so it makes no sense to store wealth in the dollar or dollar-based paper assets such as bonds, U.S. Treasuries, and insurance policies. The dollar-based assets in the world are headed for the trash heap! So the average person on the street should rebalance his or her paper assets with gold, silver, and other precious metals.

The Occupy movement and similar mass protests around the world point to generalized mistrust of financial institutions and government. The common man or "99 percent" are waking up to the reality that banks, large corporations and even the government have put profit and self-interest ahead of the interests of the people they serve. In other words, they have put their own interest above the interest of the individual. Some would say, "*They simply don't give a dam about little old me. I must fight for my rights as an individual or they will trample over me.*" Approval ratings of politicians and government are at historic lows with no signs of improvement.

In 2015, a new wave of anti-establishment sentiment began to take hold in the United States. In a wholly unpredictable turn of events, Donald Trump was elected President of the United States in January 2016. President Trump offers a fresh, new perspective in American politics by adhering to his nationalistic plan of "Make America Great Again" vis-à-vis the rest of the world.

Mr. Trump has enacted a tax plan that would completely eliminate federal taxes for those families earning less than $50,000 per year, caps the highest tax bracket—those who earn more than $250,000 per year—at 25%, and reduces the corporate tax rate to 15%. He is definitely taking some steps in the direction of making the United States government more solvent, but even "the Donald" may not be able to stop the tsunami of financial turmoil that is sure to accompany the ***dollar implosion*** followed by the ***return of the Gold Standard.***

However, Americans still believe in the core values of hard work and family. They are rapidly learning that the key to preserving wealth is by storing it in tangible assets such as gold and silver. Americans want to keep the fruits of their labor, rather than give them away to the U.S. government and Wall Street. The return of the Gold Standard will certainly help maintain the economic value of money for the average person, rather than tacitly allowing the Federal Reserve and other central banks to inflate away the value of their currency.

The financial pundits and Wall Street claim that they have the correct strategy for managing your money. They will vehemently proclaim, until their last breath, that you are making a big mistake. But you know that they do not have your best interest in mind. They do not care if your entire life savings dwindles away to nothing, because they continue to live off of your wealth. ***Remember-- preserve your wealth by shifting your dollar-based assets such as stocks, bonds and annuities into gold, silver and commodities!***

For More Information,
Please Visit www.DollarImplosion.com.

CHAPTER 11
PARADIGM SHIFT

The significance of the collapse of the dollar cannot be overstated. It will affect the lives of every human being on earth. However, this monumental event in history must be viewed in the context of a larger paradigm shift from the Industrial Age to the Age of the Individual. Only when viewed from this larger perspective does the inevitable collapse of the "Almighty Dollar" make sense.

In fact, it makes perfect sense that when the dollar collapses, a broader, more balanced worldview that harmonizes the material world with the spiritual should take its place. But the term "spiritual" is laden with a multitude of meaning. For the purposes of this book, the spiritual world can simply be defined as the relationship of the individual with the universe.

This "spiritual" worldview, by definition, places the most importance upon individual feelings, perception, and viewpoint. The individual perspective becomes paramount in this new paradigm or worldview. Hence, the paradigm shift to the **Age of the Individual**.

Many scholars have postulated theories of how the individual perspective can be the ultimate reality. Physicist David Bohm, Stanford Neuropsychologist Karl Pribram and Stanford Engineering Professor Willis Harman have all made important contributions to establishing the framework for the new paradigm--the Age of the Individual.

DAVID BOHM—"HOLOGRAPHIC MODEL"

American-born physicist David Bohm developed the holographic model of the universe. A hologram is a three-dimensional image created by the intersection of lasers, in which even the tiniest division of the whole image contains the same information as the whole.

The principle behind the hologram is a very powerful principle that we are just beginning to understand. In essence, each building block contains the same unifying information as the larger whole.

One of Bohm's most startling assertions is that the tangible reality of our everyday lives is really a kind of illusion, like a holographic image. Underlying it is a deeper order of existence, a vast and more primary level of reality that gives birth to all the objects and appearances of our physical world, in much the same way that a piece of holographic film gives birth to a hologram. (Wikipedia, "David Bohm," http://en.wikipedia.org/wiki/David_Bohm (accessed February 16, 2012))

Bohm calls this deeper level of reality--**the implicate** (which means enfolded or hidden) **order**, and he refers to our own level of existence as the explicate, or unfolded order. Put another way, electrons and all other particles are no more substantive or permanent than the form a geyser of water takes as it gushes out of a fountain. They are sustained by a constant influx from the implicate order and when a particle appears to be destroyed, it is not lost. It has merely enfolded back into the deeper order from which it sprang.

Bohm postulates that the ultimate nature of physical reality is not a collection of separate objects (as it appears to us), but rather it is an undivided whole that is in perpetual dynamic flux. For Bohm, the insights of quantum mechanics and relativity theory point to a universe that is undivided and in which all parts merge and unite in one totality. According to the holographic principle of the universe, even the smallest particles contain all of the information of the universe. This is the unifying principle of the universe that physicists have finally discovered.

By analogy, our individual consciousness is directly linked to the larger universal consciousness. This is what is meant by the spiritual masters when they state that you can achieve anything that you put your mind to—it is because the subconscious power of the mind implicitly contains and is directly connected to all of the information in the larger holographic universe.

KARL PRIBRAM—"HOLONOMIC BRAIN THEORY"

Working independently in the field of brain research, Stanford neuropsychologist Karl Pribram also became persuaded by the concept of the holographic nature of reality. He believes that the human brain can be modeled as a hologram. Pribram was drawn to the holographic model by the puzzle of how and where memories are stored in the brain.

For decades, numerous studies have shown that rather than being confined to a specific location, memories are dispersed throughout the brain. In a series of landmark experiments in the 1920s, brain scientist Karl Lashley found that no matter what portion of a rat's brain he removed, he was unable to eradicate its memory of how to perform complex tasks it had learned prior to surgery.

The only problem was that no one was able to come up with a mechanism that might explain this curious whole-in-every-part nature of memory storage. Then in the 1960s, Pribram encountered the concept of holography, and realized he had found the explanation for which brain scientists had been searching.

He believes memories are encoded not in neurons, or small groupings of neurons, but in patterns of nerve impulses that crisscross the entire brain in the same way that patterns of laser light interference crisscross the entire area of a piece of film containing a holographic image.

Our brains are our windows of perception. Each mind always contains the whole picture, but with a limited and unclear perspective. We each have different experience in our lives, but each perspective is valid. Our brains mathematically construct objective reality by interpreting frequencies that are ultimately projections from another dimension, a deeper order of existence that is beyond both space and time. (Wikipedia, "David Bohm," http://en.wikipedia.org/wiki/David_Bohm (accessed February 16, 2012))

The late Willis Harman, PhD, who was a Stanford professor of engineering and past president of the Institute of Noetic Sciences in Sausalito, California, discusses these ideas in his brilliant audio program *Insight into the New Age.* Dr. Harman sums it up this way: ***"The new paradigm of human society is based on the primacy of inner conscious awareness as a causal reality."***

This concept is revolutionary because it states that we actually create the world around us with our thoughts and actions. This is the paradigm of the Age of the Individual. If we accept this paradigm as true, we can say that thinking or meditating is actually helping to transform the world! So we all help to create whatever we focus our thoughts and energies upon.

We are now living through a paradigm shift in our collective worldview. We are moving from a scientific, deterministic worldview centered on the material world to a consciousness-based worldview that balances the inner world of consciousness with the outer material world--the Age of the Individual. In fact, the ***primacy*** of our thoughts and awareness is actually the driving force behind the reality we are living.

This means that we now recognize that we as individuals can be, do or have anything by first creating it in our thoughts! This is revolutionary when compared to the old paradigm of determinism. Many of us were taught that there is an objective world that takes precedence over any one particular subjective viewpoint. But the new paradigm turns the old paradigm on its head by stating the subjective viewpoint of each and every being not only contributes to the objective reality but actually creates that reality.

In fact, everything in your life today has been attracted or created by you through your thoughts and emotions. This is an awesome ability and responsibility that each and every one of us possesses. You can create whatever it is you desire in your life through your "inner conscious awareness"—your thoughts and emotions. Your wish is the universe's command.

As more and more individuals utilize the awesome power of their conscious and unconscious mind to rapidly bring about positive change in their lives, society reaches a tipping point when the new paradigm takes root and becomes accepted as the norm of human thought and behavior. As we evolve individually in our day-to-day existence, so too do we evolve collectively as a species.

The United Nations Summit in New York in September 2015 set forth the most ambitious goals for its member nations in the history of the organization. These Sustainable Development Goals follow and expand on the millennium development goals which were agreed on by governments in 2001 and are set to expire at the end of 2015. As the MDG deadline approaches, about 1 billion people still live on less than $1.25 a day (the World Bank measure on poverty) and more than 800 million people do not have enough food to eat.

Here is the list of the United Nations Sustainable Development Goals adopted in September 2015:

1) End poverty in all its forms everywhere
2) End hunger, achieve food security and improved nutrition and promote sustainable agriculture
3) Ensure healthy lives and promote well-being for all at all ages
4) Ensure inclusive and equitable quality education and promote lifelong learning opportunities for all
5) Achieve gender equality and empower all women and girls
6) Ensure availability and sustainable management of water and sanitation for all
7) Ensure access to affordable, reliable, sustainable and modern energy for all
8) Promote sustained, inclusive and sustainable economic growth, full and productive employment and decent work for all
9) Build resilient infrastructure, promote inclusive and sustainable industrialization and foster innovation
10) Reduce inequality within and among countries
11) Make cities and human settlements inclusive, safe, resilient and sustainable

12) Ensure sustainable consumption and production patterns
13) Take urgent action to combat climate change and its impacts
14) Conserve and sustainably use the oceans, seas and marine resources for sustainable development
15) Protect, restore and promote sustainable use of terrestrial ecosystems, sustainably manage forests, combat desertification, and halt and reverse land degradation and halt biodiversity loss
16) Promote peaceful and inclusive societies for sustainable development, provide access to justice for all and build effective, accountable and inclusive institutions at all levels
17) Strengthen the means of implementation and revitalize the Global Partnership for Sustainable Development

(United Nations website, Sustainable Development Goals, http://www.un.org/ga/search/view_doc.asp?symbol=A/69/L.85&Lang=E, (accessed October 6, 2015))

These goals are broad in scope and extremely ambitious. For the first time in history, the collective consciousness of humanity may be able to bring an end to poverty and hunger on a global scale. All human beings should indeed have access to quality education, gender equality, water and sanitation, affordable energy, productive employment, infrastructure, and safety.

The Sustainable Development Goals also include environmental goals such as combating climate change, protecting the oceans and marine resources, and protecting terrestrial ecosystems. When enough attention and resources are directed toward these goals, they shall be attained for our sake and for the sake of generations to come.

If this paradigm is true, then each individual advertently or inadvertently has a direct impact on the universe, beyond geographical and temporal boundaries. This may be why live sporting events are so popular throughout the world.

In other words, if the holographic paradigm is valid, spectators of sporting events may have a small but direct impact on the outcome of the sporting event, whether watching the event live or on television, by focusing their attention or consciousness on the event. It is the holographic interconnectedness of the universe that allows one person or event to have a direct impact on another person or event, even though they may be separated by space and time.

Synchronicity is another term for the interconnectedness of the universe. Why have major milestones in human history occurred in different places at around the same time? For instance, why was human slavery abolished throughout the world in the 1860s? Perhaps, the concept of freedom from slavery was manifesting itself throughout the universe at that point in history. The holographic interconnectivity of the universe thus explains why major advances in human history have occurred contemporaneously in disparate places around the planet.

In his delightful book *The Instant Millionaire*, Mark Fisher presents a memorable fable of a young man who learns from a millionaire gardener the keys to a happy and prosperous life. The millionaire's secret was,

> *"The world is but a reflection of your inner self. The conditions in your life are but a mirror image of your inner life... Like everyone else, your self-image is so powerful that it unwittingly becomes your destiny. Outer circumstances end up matching the image you have of yourself with*

amazing precision. To become rich, you have to create a new self-image. "(Fisher 1990, 71–75)

This is why affirmations are so important in programming our minds and creating our future—because they help to shape our self-image, the blueprint of our lives. The millionaire also gave the young man another secret to happiness. He told the young man that when life seems unbearable, repeat the following affirmation, *"Be still, and know that I am God."* This can be interpreted to mean that all human beings are a reflection of God, and are entitled to God-given peace and tranquility. We simply have to remind ourselves of our own godliness from time to time.

In this way, we are all creating our individual and collective futures. We not only create our own reality, but we help to create the reality of the universe. This is truly profound. The next time we hear someone say that they do not matter much in the grand scheme of things, we can respond by saying that they matter profoundly to the entire universe.

It is no coincidence that the U.S. dollar is imploding at the same time that the paradigm shift from the Industrial Age to the Age of the Individual is occurring. The dollar is the iconic symbol of material wealth in the world. However, the importance of the material world is now giving way to the primacy of *individual consciousness* as a causal reality.

Therefore, the dollar and the entire materialistic bent of the American empire must make room for spiritual traditions which are deeply rooted in Far Eastern cultures. The dollar will soon implode, allowing a more balanced global economic system to manifest itself. With the newfound understanding of the dollar collapse as part of a much larger global transformation to the Age of the Individual, **now** is the time to make the necessary changes in your financial plan for the future.

Great benefits arise from the awakening of the collective consciousness. Human beings are able to focus their collective energy on heretofore unsolved global problems like hunger, poverty, and global warming. Nations now learn from each other with ever-increasing speed, hastening the maturation of each and every nation's economy and, as a result, the global economy.

The United States has played a crucial role in this phase of our human evolution—it has unified the far corners of the world into one vast global economy primarily based on the Anglo-Saxon business model. Ultimately, the United States will have to relinquish the role of global unifier, but will continue to be a major player in the global economy. This is because no one nation or people can control a multipolar global economy, as we shall learn this decade.

In fact, the evolution of our species paradoxically means the devolution of power from large nations and organizations to the *individual*. The individual is the microcosm of humanity, and thereby must possess all of the powers that great nations have possessed in the past. This is the global transformation we are now living through--the transformation from the Industrial Age to the globally interconnected **Age of the Individual**.

In addition, the nations of the world are more dependent on each other than ever before. The degree of interconnectivity is increasing exponentially with increasing trade and more and more technology binding the human race together.

For example, the United States now relies heavily on cheaper goods and services from China to maintain its high standard of living. But China relies heavily on the United States and the West to purchase its products to keep up its rapid rate of growth. Neither the United States nor China wishes to see the other fail, because they each rely on the other. It is in each nation's own interest to see other nations become more prosperous.

If there is lack of growth or stagnation, it is because inherent imbalances in the system require rectification. The United States has a serious spending problem that requires correction, but the correction will not come from the politicians in power. It will be forced on the United States by the very system the United States has fought so mightily to spread around the world, the free market system. The coming dollar implosion will force the American empire into submission to the global world order which it helped create...

For More Information
Please Visit www.DollarImplosion.com.

CHAPTER 12

INDIVIDUAL EMPOWERMENT

The financial implications of the impending dollar implosion have been discussed at length. Broad financial strategies have been put forth to help oneself prepare for and prosper during this time of financial upheaval. But the question arises, "How do those less fortunate individuals, who basically live paycheck to paycheck and do not have any funds to invest, prepare for and prosper during the coming dollar implosion and paradigm shift to the Age of the Individual?"

Actually, financial preparedness is only one manner of preparing oneself for the coming changes in our society. **The Age of the Individual is about empowering oneself to realize one's life ambitions and dreams**. Almost by definition, this new age must address the totality of human existence. Individual empowerment can be broken down into the following components: the body, the mind, and the spirit. In other words, we must nourish ourselves in the physical, mental, and spiritual realms.

All human beings, even poor people or those of lesser means, can benefit from learning new strategies of improving one's life. I would like to offer the reader a brief overview of some individual empowerment strategies, some of which I have personally benefited from. By no means is this an exhaustive list of strategies. I leave it to the reader to make his or her own judgment as to the value of these strategies and whether or not to utilize them. Let's first touch upon some important concepts regarding physical health.

Individuals create their own reality--including their health. In Greek mythology, one of the most famous ancient riddles of the Sphinx was, "What has one voice and yet becomes four-footed, two-footed and three-footed?" Oedipus gave the obvious answer: the human being. The human being crawls on all fours during infancy, walks on two legs as an adult, and then leans on a cane during old age. Old age was and is equated with debility.

As we age, a gradual, relentless degenerative process occurs. But what makes some people age at a different rate than others? Can the aging process be slowed down? These are age-old questions that deserve some attention. Traditional allopathic medicine teaches us that there are "risk factors," both uncontrollable and controllable, for heart disease. The uncontrollable risk factors include age, gender, and family history. The controllable risk factors include high blood pressure, high cholesterol, sedentary living, obesity, cigarette smoking, and stress.

Stephen T. Sinatra, MD, cardiologist and author of *Optimum Health* (1996), takes a holistic approach to aging, disease, and health. He believes that aging is a disease process, and subscribes to the free radical theory of the aging of cells, "Aging, in simple terms, is related to the accumulated damage to membranes and cells as a consequence of oxidative stress. The metabolism of oxygen results in the formation of free radicals. A free radical is a molecule with an odd number of electrons, a negatively charged particle." (Sinatra 1996, 134)

During the process known as oxidative metabolism, which occurs via a chemical pathway known as reduction, oxygen is "reduced" to water by the sequential addition of four electrons, which results in generation of free radical molecules with high reactivity. Free radical generation reaches much higher levels during situations of extraordinary radical flux such as infection, inflammation, radiation exposure, and high oxygen tension states such as during vigorous exercise or "heart attack." He even goes as far as saying that premature heart disease and various forms of cancer, autoimmune diseases, and Alzheimer's disease are really entities of premature aging.

Dr. Sinatra's stated mission is "to make people aware of how they can directly optimize their health, ward off disease and live a healthier life. By raising consciousness and initiating a healthy preventive lifestyle, individuals can literally prevent premature aging and the diseases of this century." His approach is convincing because he approaches the concept of disease holistically—that healing can and should be approached on the physical, psychological, and spiritual levels concomitantly. He states that the common denominators for longevity appear to include (1) a low-fat, high fiber diet, (2) exercise, and (3) supportive, loving relationships.

Simply put, a healthy diet and daily exercise are crucial to a healthy life. A healthy diet means plenty of fruits and vegetables; Americans do not consume enough fruits and vegetables. They have been duped by the food industry to the effect that processed foods are sufficient for a healthy lifestyle. My father, an internist, always told us that you must eat at least seven fruits and vegetables a day. I believe he was right.

In fact, a whole new mega-industry has developed around the concept of wellness. Paul Zane Pilzer outlines the opportunities for anybody who wishes to take part in this exciting new industry in his outstanding book, *The Wellness Revolution (2002)*. He asserts that the health and wellness industry is here to stay and will be the next trillion dollar industry. He states that the sickness business is "*reactive*" while the wellness business is "*proactive*." "People voluntarily become customers—to feel healthier, to reduce the effects of aging, and to avoid becoming customers of the sickness business." (Pilzer 2002, 4)

The mental realm of our existence relies heavily on the power of the subconscious and on our self-image. As discussed earlier, our self-image essentially determines our reality. The outer circumstances of our life conform to our inner life and self-image with amazing precision. The subconscious is the key to manifesting our self-image.

We can change our reality by commanding our subconscious to change our self-image. This process has been given myriad names including cybernetics, affirmation, positive thinking, and positive mental attitude. All of these techniques rely on programming our subconscious through the repetition of words and images.

The French physician Emile Coue created a famous affirmation for improving health and well-being, "Every day in every way, I am getting better and better." This is a simple but very effective affirmation. Affirmations are one of the most effective ways of programming the subconscious mind to achieve one's goals.

The subconscious can be programmed for quite specific results as well. The millionaire gardener in the *Instant Millionaire* by Mark Fisher details how specifically to program the young man's subconscious to enable him to become a millionaire. He states that first one needs a quantified objective. Next, one must repeat a specific formula to oneself aloud at least fifty times a day to effectively program the subconscious. The young man then came up with the formula, "I will earn $32,000 next year. I will double my income every year for the next six years so that I will become a millionaire on _____." Repetition is the key to programming one's subconscious.

Visualization is another powerful tool to utilize in programming one's subconscious. If one desires to be wealthy, he or she should devote time every day to visualizing himself or herself living the life of a wealthy person. Guided imagery is another technique of relaxation which relies on the power of visual images. Cancer patients have used this technique with much success, visualizing their body's immune system attacking and destroying the rapidly multiplying cancer cells. Athletes use visualization to perfect their stroke or technique.

The most effective method of actually creating your reality is to spend 15 to 20 minutes a day imaging your life exactly the way you desire it to be, according to Abraham in *The Law of Attraction* by Esther and Jerry Hicks. Abraham calls this the Creative Workshop and teaches the reader that anything that he or she desires must manifest itself by the Law of Attraction, but it must be visualized with emotion. It must be believed and expected. It must then be allowed to manifest itself.

Lucid dreaming is another technique of exploring the subconscious world. The term "lucid dream" was coined by Dutch psychiatrist Frederik van Eeden; it means that the dreamer becomes aware that he or she is dreaming, and can manipulate the experiences in the dream environment. Lucid dreaming is a skill that can be learned, similar to learning a new language. However, it requires lots of practice.

According to Far Eastern spiritual teachings, each soul, Atman, longs to unite itself with the larger universal soul, Brahman. This is similar to an individual wave on the ocean becoming one with the vastly larger ocean. The ancient rishis of India calculated that it would take one million years of disease-free evolution for a soul to achieve union with the Infinite. So they set out to develop a superfast method of achieving union with the Infinite in one lifetime and called it yoga. There are many different kinds of yoga including Hatha Yoga, Kundalini Yoga, Raja Yoga and Kriya Yoga.

In 1920, Paramahansa Yogananda formed the Self Realization Fellowship in Los Angeles, California and played a large role in introducing yoga to the West. This organization is dedicated to disseminating the teachings of Yogananda to earnest spiritual seekers. In 1946, Yogananda published his life story, *Autobiography of a Yogi*, which introduced many westerners to meditation and yoga. It has since been translated into twenty-five languages and the various editions published since its inception have sold over a million copies worldwide. (Wikipedia, "Paramahansa Yogananda," http://en.wikipedia.org/wiki/Paramahansa_Yogananda (accessed February 16, 2012))

Many other spiritual teachings are available to sincere seekers. Transcendental Meditation (TM) is another technique of meditation, espoused by Maharishi Mahesh Yogi from the 1960s and onward. More recently, Harold Benson from Harvard University coined the term "relaxation response" and discussed its beneficial effects on those who utilize his techniques of relaxation. The bottom line is that meditation and prayer are enormously beneficial on all levels-- the physical, mental and spiritual.

More recently, Esther and Jerry Hicks have authored *The Law of Attraction: The Basics of the Teachings of Abraham*, a sort of new age guide to practical spirituality. In this book, Esther Hicks channels a group of beings called Abraham who answers Jerry's questions about life. Abraham states emphatically that each and every individual human being has created their own unique life experience through their thought. He goes on to assert that every individual can consciously create and live the life that they want to live by understanding and applying the three Eternal Universal Laws: (1) the *Law of Attraction*, (2) the *Science of Deliberate Creation*, and (3) the *Art of Allowing*.

Throughout the ages, those individuals of great wealth and power have known about and utilized this principle and tried to keep it a secret. But the secret is so simple it seems like child's play—and it is. Here are the three simple steps for creating whatever it is you desire:

Step 1: ASK—Ask for what you want. You do this consciously and unconsciously throughout your waking life. In Abraham's words, you are constantly sending out "rockets of desire" into the universe. For example, when someone is rude to you, you want them to be nicer. This is the "CAUSE."

Step 2: IT IS GIVEN—The universe responds to your "rocket of desire" by creating what you desire in the nonphysical, vibrational realm. This is not your work—this is the Universal Law at work. This is the "EFFECT."

Step 3: ALLOW AND RECEIVE—This is *your work*. In other words, it is your job to come into complete alignment with your desire. This means you have to feel as if you have already achieved your desire. **This is the crucial and most difficult part of manifesting your desires**.

So how does one "align" with his or her desires? One extremely powerful method of achieving vibrational alignment with your desires is to utilize the technique of chanting "Nam Myoho Renge

Kyo" as taught by Nichiren Buddhism. This phrase roughly translates into "Devotion to the Mystic Law of Simultaneous Cause and Effect of the Universe." According to the philosophy of Nichiren Buddhism, the entire Lotus Sutra can be boiled down to the simple phrase, "Nam Myoho Renge Kyo." Nichiren teaches that this phrase encompasses all laws and teachings within itself and that the benefit of chanting "Nam Myoho Renge Kyo" includes the benefit of conducting all virtuous practices. (Ikeda 2013, 418) Although the topic of Buddhism is too vast to begin to address in this work, suffice it say that this technique of chanting is very effective in helping one achieve alignment with one's desires.

The infinite power of the universe will give you what you want if you follow these steps. We have all come to planet Earth to make our dreams come true. It is high time we all grasp the incredible power of our mind and thoughts upon the material universe in which we live. It's time we reaffirm our inherent birthright as creators. . .

EPILOGUE

The United States government is analogous to the larger American empire itself. It will not shrink on its own. There must be a major crisis for this to happen. The crisis is the coming **dollar implosion**— and it will be the beginning of an historical transformation to a more globally integrated political and economic system.

At the same time, it will be the birth of the individual empowerment society and the **Age of the Individual**. The common man will no longer require government to make decisions for him. He will live in a world of personal and professional empowerment--a world that works for everyone.

The arguments for the imminent implosion of the U.S. dollar and the eventual return of the Gold Standard have been presented in a very straightforward manner for the common man so that he may take heed and prepare for the day of reckoning!

I hope that you utilize the concepts presented in this book for spiritual, mental, physical, and financial prosperity. If any of the concepts or predictions has moved you to make positive changes in your life, then I will have succeeded in my mission to elevate the well-being of humanity.

For More Information
Please Visit www.DollarImplosion.com.

BIBLIOGRAPHY

Ali, Abdullah Yusuf, trans. *The Qur'an: Text, Translation, and Commentary (English and Arabic Edition)*. Elmhurst, NY: Tahrike Tarsile Qur'an, 2001.

Arguelles, Jose. *The Mayan Factor: Path Beyond Technology*. Rochester, VT: Bear & Company, 1987.

Bohm, David and B.J. Hiley. *The Undivided Universe: An Ontological Interpretation of Quantum Theory*. New York: Routledge, 1993.

Bowman, Joel. "Consumer Spending and the Decline of the U.S. Economy." *The Daily Reckoning*, May 13, 2011. http://wwwdailyreckoning.com/consumer-spending-and-the-decline-of-the-us-economy (accessed February 16, 2012).

Casey, Douglas. *Crisis Investing: Opportunities and Profits in the Coming Great Depression*. New York: HarperCollins, 1980.

Clark, William. *Petrodollar Warfare: Oil, Iraq and Future of the Dollar*. Gabriola Island, British Columbia: New Society Publishers, 2005.

Fisher, Mark. *The Instant Millionaire: A Tale of Wisdom and Wealth*. Novato, CA: New World Library, 1990.

Goodman, Al. "Thousands of Spaniards Call for Economic Reform in New Protest." *CNN World*, June 19, 2011. http://www.cnn.com/2011/WORLD/europe/06/19/spain.protests/index.html (accessed February 16, 2012).

Harman, Willis. *Global Mind Change: The Promise of the 21ˢᵗ Century.* San Francisco, CA: Berrett-Koehler Publishers, 1998.

———*Insight into the New Age* (audiocassette). Palo Alto, CA: Twenty-First Century Publications, 1988.

Hicks, Esther and Jerry. *The Law of Attraction.* Carlsbad, CA: Hay House Inc., 2006.

Ikeda, Daisaku. *The Heart of the Lotus Sutra.* Santa Monica, CA: World Tribune Press, 2013.

Johnson, Chalmers. *The Sorrows of Empire.* New York: Metropolitan Books/Henry Holt and Company, 2004.

Kubler-Ross, Elisabeth. *On Death and Dying.* New York: Simon & Schuster, 1969.

Le Gai Eaton, Charles. *The Book of Hadith: Sayings of the Prophet Muhammad from the Mishkat al Masabih.* Watsonville, CA: The Book Foundation, 2008.

Pilzer, Paul. *The Wellness Revolution.* Hoboken, NJ: John Wiley & Sons, 2002.

Pribram, Karl. *Brain and Perception: Holonomy and Structure in Figural Processing.* Florence, KY: Psychology Press, 1991.

Rickards, James. *The Death of Money: The Coming Collapse of the International Monetary System.* New York: Portfolio/Penguin, 2014.

Rivers, Tom. "Thousands of Irish Protest Austerity Measures." *Voice of America News*, November 27, 2010. http://www.voanews.com/english/news/Thousands-of-Irish-Protest-Austerity-Measures-110904779.html (accessed February 16, 2012).

Sinatra, Stephen. *Optimum Health: A Natural Lifesaving Prescription for Your Body and Mind.* New York: Bantam Books, 1997.

Talbot, Michael. *The Holographic Universe.* New York: HarperCollins, 1991.

Tapscott, Don and Anthony Williams. *Wikinomics: How Mass Collaboration Changes Everything.* New York: Portfolio/Penguin Group, 2008.

Turk, James and John Rubino. *The Coming Collapse of the Dollar and How to Profit from It: Make a Fortune by Investing in Gold and Other Hard Assets.* New York: Doubleday, 2004.

Unger, Craig. *House of Bush, House of Saud: The Secret Relationship Between the World's Two Most Powerful Dynasties.* New York: Scribner, 2004.

Wiedemer, David et al. *Aftershock: Protect Yourself and Profit in the Next Global Financial Meltdown.* Hoboken, NJ: John Wiley & Sons, 2010.

Willie, Jim. *The Hat Trick Letter.* www.goldenjackass.com.

World Bank. *Global Development Horizons 2011: Multipolarity—The New Global Economy.* Washington, DC: The International Bank for Reconstruction and Development/The World Bank, 2011.

Yogananda, Paramahansa. *Autobiography of a Yogi.* New York: The Philosophical Library, 1946.

Printed in the United States
By Bookmasters